TRANSFORMING LITERACY EDUCATION FOR LONG-TERM ENGLISH LEARNERS

Grounded in research on bilingualism and adolescent literacy, this volume provides a much-needed insight into the day-to-day needs of students who are identified as long-term English learners (LTELs). LTELs are adolescents who are primarily or solely educated in the U.S. and yet remain identified as "learning English" in secondary school. Challenging the deficit perspective that is often applied to their experiences of language learning, Brooks counters incorrect characterizations of LTELs and sheds light on students' strengths to argue that effective literacy education requires looking beyond policy classifications that are often used to guide educational decisions for this population.

By combining research, theory, and practice, this book offers a comprehensive analysis of literacy pedagogy to facilitate teacher learning and includes practical takeaways and implications for classroom practice and professional development. Offering a pathway for transforming literacy education for students identified as LTELs, chapters discuss reframing the education of LTELs, academic reading in the classroom, and the bilingualism of students who are labeled LTELs.

Transforming Literacy Education for Long-term English Learners is a much-needed resource for scholars, professors, researchers, and graduate students in language and literacy education, English education, and teacher education, and for those who are looking to create an inclusive and successful classroom environment for LTELs.

Maneka Deanna Brooks is an Assistant Professor of Reading Education at Texas State University, USA.

NCTE-Routledge Research Series

Series Editors: Valerie Kinloch and Susi Long

Alsup
Teacher Identity Discourses: Negotiating Personal and Professional Spaces

Banks
Race, Rhetoric, and Technology: Searching for Higher Ground

Daniell/Mortensen
Women and Literacy: Local and Global Inquiries for a New Century

Rickford/Sweetland/Rickford/Grano
African American, Creole and other Vernacular Englishes in Education: A Bibliographic Resource

Guerra
Language, Culture, Identity, and Citizenship in College Classrooms and Communities

Haddix
Cultivating Racial and Linguistic Diversity in Literacy Teacher Education: Teachers Like Me

Brooks
Transforming Literacy Education for Long-term English Learners: Recognizing Brilliance in the Undervalued

The NCTE-Routledge Research Series, copublished by the National Council of Teachers of English and Routledge, focuses on literacy studies in P-12 classroom and related contexts. Volumes in this series are invited publications or publications submitted in response to a call for manuscripts. They are primarily authored or co-authored works which are theoretically significant and broadly relevant to the P-12 literacy community. The series may also include occasional landmark compendiums of research.

The scope of the series includes qualitative and quantitative methodologies; a range of perspectives and approaches (e.g., sociocultural, cognitive, feminist, linguistic, pedagogical, critical, historical, anthropological); and research on diverse populations, contexts (e.g., classrooms, school systems, families, communities), and forms of literacy (e.g., print, electronic, popular media).

TRANSFORMING LITERACY EDUCATION FOR LONG-TERM ENGLISH LEARNERS

Recognizing Brilliance in the Undervalued

Maneka Deanna Brooks

Routledge
Taylor & Francis Group

NEW YORK AND LONDON

A co-publication of Routledge and NCTE

First published 2020
by Routledge
52 Vanderbilt Avenue, New York, NY 10017

and by Routledge
2 Park Square, Milton Park, Abingdon, Oxon, OX14 4RN

Routledge is an imprint of the Taylor & Francis Group, an informa business

© 2020 Taylor & Francis

Library of Congress Cataloging-in-Publication Data
A catalog record for this title has been requested

ISBN: 978-1-138-55810-6 (hbk)
ISBN: 978-1-138-55811-3 (pbk)
ISBN: 978-1-315-15123-6 (ebk)

Typeset in Bembo
by Newgen Publishing UK

CONTENTS

EXPANDED TABLE OF CONTENTS

ILLUSTRATIONS

Figures

Tables

SERIES EDITORS' FOREWORD

"Miss, can you help me?" are the words that open Chapter 1 of Maneka Deanna Brooks' new book, *Transforming literacy education for long-term English learners: Recognizing brilliance in the undervalued*. These words were shared with Maneka by Santiago Flores, a high school student who was placed in an English as a Second Language (ESL) class at a large comprehensive school in Southern California. Santiago wanted Maneka, who, at the time, "was a naïve 21-year-old recent college graduate, employed as a long-term substitute teacher," to help him "get out of this class" because it was for students who needed to be more fully immersed in learning to speak English. He knew that he did not belong there and he sought a way out.

In fact, Santiago already spoke English and had been doing so for almost his entire life. Yet he was placed in a class for students who needed to learn to speak the English language. Santiago also knew the challenges that come with not having an adult to advocate on behalf of his educational rights, especially when it comes to the deeply rooted racist practices, policies, and politics inherent with the institution of schooling in this country. Yet he did not have an adult who could positively advocate for him to not be in this class, as his parents did not speak English and found it difficult to communicate with the school counselor. Like one too many Black, Latinx, and Indigenous students who attend U.S. schools, Santiago recognized the hurdles placed in his way, hurdles that sought to define his educational trajectory by ignoring his linguistic virtuosity. Santiago turned to Maneka for help, and although she offered him suggestions (e.g., that his parents should meet with his counselor; that he, himself, could talk with the counselor), he had already tried them all to no avail. Thus, Santiago completed and turned in the course assignment for the day, but Maneka never saw him again.

SHE NEVER SAW SANTIAGO AGAIN! However, her brief encounter with Santiago has highly impacted the direction she takes with regards to her research and teaching. According to Maneka, "In the 15 years since my initial interaction with Santiago, I have dedicated my life to creating affirming and academically rigorous learning environments for students who are considered to be long-term English learners (LTELs)." This point comes through so powerfully and beautifully in the critical, humanizing, and loving stories Maneka shares in this book about the brilliance and bravery of five adolescent Latinx students—Destiny, Eliza, Lizbeth, Jamilet, and Valeria—who have been labeled English learners since kindergarten. Even more powerful is how Maneka, herself, sees students (and, in this case, LTELs) as agentive human beings who have every right to literacy opportunities that allow them to both survive and thrive in schools and in the larger world. For us (Valerie and Susi), this is an important takeaway from her book. Additionally, the power of educators to *really* learn about and listen to LTEL students, and to recognize that they already have multifaceted, creative, and rich linguistic abilities are necessary to truly transform literacy education. Thank you, Maneka, for extending and adding to the current literature on LTELS, literacy education, and language studies.

Transforming literacy education for long-term English learners: Recognizing brilliance in the undervalued is a must-read. Like the other books in our NCTE-Routledge Research Series, this book is concerned with the sociocultural nature of literacy practices and the ways in which literacy research and practice must attend to the lives of People of Color inside P-12 literacy classrooms and within communities. The scope of books in our series includes an explicit focus on equity, justice, and antiracist literacy education; critical qualitative, quantitative, and mixed methodologies; a range of cutting-edge perspectives and approaches (e.g., sociocultural, cognitive, feminist, linguistic, pedagogical, critical, historical, anthropological); and research on the literacies of minoritized peoples as well as on diverse contexts (e.g., classrooms, school systems, families, communities) and forms of literacy (e.g., print, electronic, popular media).

We hope you are moved by Maneka Deanna Brooks' new book just as much as you are by the many other books in our series.

Valerie and Susi

Valerie Kinloch (vkinloch@pitt.edu)
Renée and Richard Goldman Dean and Professor
School of Education
University of Pittsburgh
and
Susi Long (susilong52@gmail.com)
Professor, Department of Instruction and Teacher Education
College of Education
University of South Carolina, Columbia

1

MORE THAN LONG-TERM ENGLISH LEARNERS

Reframing the Education of an Under-served Population

Miss, can you help me?

Santiago Flores

While all the other students were working in small groups, Santiago Flores[1] laid his head on the table. When I approached him, he looked up and asked, "Miss, can you help me?" I sat down at the table to answer his questions about the assignment. However, rather than discussing the assignment, he said, "I need to get out of this class. I speak English and no one else here does." His statement shocked me. I was a naïve 21-year-old recent college graduate, employed as a long-term substitute teacher for an English as a Second Language (ESL) class at a large comprehensive high school in Southern California. I did not understand how someone who was speaking English to me could be in a class whose primary purpose was the teaching and learning of English.

After Santiago shared with me that he spoke English and that he had been speaking English for most of his life, I did not know how to help him. So, I suggested the first two ideas that immediately came to mind. My first suggestion was that his parents talk to his counselor. He explained that his parents did not speak English, and they struggled to communicate with his counselor. I asked him how it was possible that he and his parents spoke two different languages. He said that he usually spoke to his parents in English, and they spoke to him in Spanish. My second suggestion was for him to talk to his counselor himself. However, he quickly clarified that he had already tried this tactic and that the counselor said that his English reading test scores were not good enough. I did not have any other suggestions for Santiago, so I encouraged him to complete the assignment, and I began circling the room to answer other students' questions. At the end of the class period, he turned in the completed assignment and left. I never saw Santiago again.

As a long-term substitute teacher who had yet to go through a teacher education program, my inability to recognize Santiago's situation was situated in the fact that I knew very little about bilingualism, how students officially came to be classified as English learners (ELs) in school, and how this classification could impact their course placement. Moreover, I was raised in an English-speaking home, which meant that the lived experience of being a bilingual student in U.S. schools was unknown to me. As a result, my encounter with Santiago initially felt like an anomaly. It was a random error that lead to a student with a unique linguistic life to be placed in an incorrect class. Even though it appeared to me that Santiago's course placement was happenstance, my interaction with him remained in my mind for years to come. I wondered about how such a grievous error could have occurred. I wondered how Santiago, who was someone who self-identified as an English-speaker and spoke English, was not able to exit from ESL.

As my career in education progressed, I learned that Santiago's experience as an English-speaking student who was classified as an *English learner* (EL) and placed in specific courses to learn English was not an isolated instance (Brooks, 2019; Bryan, Cooper, & Infarinu, 2019; Motha, 2014). Students who are classified as ELs (see Figure 1.1 for federal definition of EL) are legally entitled to an educational environment that provides with them with the opportunity to both learn English and academic content (Haas & Gort, 2009). For Santiago, as with other students with similar linguistic backgrounds (Callahan & Shifrer, 2016; Kim & García, 2014; Menken & Kleyn, 2010), one of the ways in which these linguistic support services were provided was through an ESL course. When I transitioned from my position as a long-term substitute to a full-time teacher who was enrolled in a teacher education program, many of the students who I taught reminded me of Santiago. They spoke English on a daily basis and English was an integral part of their linguistic identity; however, they remained classified as ELs. In searching for more information about this student population, I soon learned that Santiago and many of the other students that I was teaching were frequently referred to as *long-term English learners* (Freeman, Freeman, & Mercuri, 2002).

Who are Long-term English Learners?

In the 15 years since my initial interaction with Santiago, I have dedicated my life to creating affirming and academically rigorous learning environments for students who are considered to be long-term English learners (LTELs). Unlike popular conceptions of adolescent ELs as recent immigrants, LTEL students are not new to the United States or to the English language. In fact, it is the number of years that this group of young people has spent in U.S. schools that differentiates them from other adolescent ELs who are newcomers to the United States and/ or have limited formal schooling experiences. The minimum number of years a student must be classified as an EL and/or have received special language services varies between five and seven years (e.g., California Education Code §313.1;

**Excerpt from the Every Students Succeeds Act of 2015 Sec. 8101.
[20 U.S.C. 7801]**

(20) ENGLISH LEARNER.—The term "English learner", when used with respect
to an individual, means an individual—

    (A) who is aged 3 through 21;

    (B) who is enrolled or preparing to enroll in an elementary school or secondary
school;

    (C)(i) who was not born in the United States or whose native language is a
language other than English;

      (ii)(I) who is a Native American or Alaska Native, or a native resident of the
outlying areas; and

        (II) who comes from an environment where a language other than
English has had a significant impact on the individual's level of
English language proficiency; or

      (iii) who is migratory, whose native language is a language other than English,
and who comes from an environment where a language other than
English is dominant; and

    (D) whose difficulties in speaking, reading, writing, or understanding the
English language may be sufficient to deny the individual—

      (i) the ability to meet the challenging State academic standards;

      (ii) the ability to successfully achieve in classrooms where the language of
instruction is English; or

      (iii) the opportunity to participate fully in society.

FIGURE 1.1 The federal definition of English learner in the United States

New York City Department of Education, 2016; U.S. Department of Education,
2016).[2] Since there are varying definitions of what it means to be an LTEL,
there are not nationwide statistics about the demographics of this population.
For example, the state of New York identified 11.7% of their students as "long
term ELLs" during the 2015–2016 school year. In California during the 2017–
2018 school year, 17.1% were considered to be LTELs. Across the states within
the WIDA consortium, the number of projected LTELs range from 2% to 24%
(Sahakyan & Ryan, 2018).

    On the most generous end, popular descriptions of LTELs that are targeted
towards classroom teachers and others involved in education tend to acknowledge
what is often referred to as the social or oral bilingualism of this student population. Then, they qualify their description of these oral abilities through describing
their struggles with academic literacy in both languages. An article in *Educational
Leadership*, whose audience educators across grade levels, notes that LTELs "are
often orally bilingual and sound like Native English speakers. However, they typically have limited literacy skills in their native language, and their academic literacy skills in English are not as well-developed as their oral skills are" (Menken

& Kleyn, 2009). However, the dominant narrative within the practitioner-facing literature reinforces descriptions of LTELs as deficient in linguistic, literate, and academic abilities. For instance, the entry in the Glossary of Education Reform (2015) for LTELs is evidence of this perspective. It describes "[t]he defining characteristic of long-term English learners is that their English-language deficits have grown more severe and consequential over time, which has negatively affected their ability to achieve their full academic potential." In a similar vein, a publication from the National Education Association (Olsen, 2014) described LTELs as lacking the "oral and literacy skills needed for academic success" (p. 5). Another example of this type of common talk about LTELs is evidenced in Freeman et al. (2002), a book that was designed to help secondary teachers work with bilingual adolescents. They described LTELs as students who did not know how to "talk, read, and write about school subjects in their first language or in English" (p. 38).

The previously described broad and simplistic descriptions are typically situated in descriptions of LTELs' students' performance on standardized tests and belie the diversity of linguistic, literate, and academic abilities of the students to whom the LTEL label is applied. As a classroom teacher, I saw the ways in which these descriptions did not accurately characterize the students with whom I worked. Although many of my students had remained classified as English learners, usually because of their performance on standardized assessments of English literacy—which were positioned as assessments of English proficiency and/or academic achievement—I witnessed my students' multiple linguistic and literate abilities on a daily basis. For example, I taught students like Malia, who excelled in all of her classes and content area achievement tests but remained classified as an EL because of her low scores on the English language proficiency assessments. There was Gerardo, who struggled to read the textbook yet was an avid reader of anime. He could talk for hours on end in English about the intricate plotlines. Gerardo refused to participate in the assessment of his English language proficiency. He found it degrading that someone would question his English abilities. Another student, Alexis, was more disconnected from schooling than Malia or Gerardo. Yet, the rap songs in his notebook illustrated the way in which he understood how to use a variety of literary devices in English. Moreover, students' linguistic and literate abilities were not limited to English. Many of the LTEL students in my class frequently served as interpreters for family members at school, in doctors' offices, and interfacing with government agencies (e.g., Dorner, Faulstich Orellana, & Jiménez, 2008). They smoothly moved between Spanish, English, and a mixture of both languages to engage in complex tasks.

Classroom-based research that has been published in peer-reviewed journals provides another perspective of students that simplistic descriptions of LTELs based on results of standardized test scores do not show. For example, Kibler et al.'s (2017) work with sixth-grade students highlighted that although all of the young people in their study were considered LTELs, they exhibited a range of ways of interacting in the classroom. Importantly, the nature of the activities with which they were presented impacted how they engaged in learning. There was not a singular pattern of communication among students who were considered to be LTELs. The practice of describing all LTELs as not having particular abilities overlooks the way in which individual histories interact with context to illustrate students' abilities. Flores, Kleyn, and Menken's (2015) research also highlights the importance of context in the ways in which students who are considered to be LTELs demonstrate their linguistic abilities. They describe how a Spanish for Native Speakers course, which was designed to support the Spanish language development of LTELs was a space in which their home linguistic practices were devalued. As a result, students were often disengaged. Flores and colleagues point out that it was not students' limited linguistic abilities, but the beliefs about language—which were shaped by racialized ideas about monolingualism and the correct type of Spanish—that contributed to student disengagement.

Kibler et al. (2017) and Flores et al. (2015) are a part of growing strand of educational research that asserts there is not a singular normative linguistic and literate profile that accompanies the LTEL label. They highlight the importance of opportunities with which students are provided to demonstrate their linguistic and literate abilities and the impact of beliefs about the various sociopolitical identities of students (e.g., race/ethnicity, immigration status, gender, etc.). In spite of the work of these and other researchers to push back against these viewpoints (Brooks, 2017; de los Ríos, 2018; Kibler & Valdés, 2016; Kleyn & Stern, 2018; Rosa, 2016; Thompson, 2015), a focus on linguistic and literate deficits characterizes the much of the easily accessible literature that is directed at teachers and other professionals involved in the day-to-day instruction of LTELs.

Damage-centered Research and LTELs

The prevalence of this language of deficiency about LTELs' language and literacy abilities is indicative of the popularity of what Tuck (2009) terms "damage-centered research" in education. She notes that this type of research "operates, even benevolently, from a theory of change that establishes harm or injury to achieve reparation" (p. 413). In situating this theory of change within the practitioner-focused literature on LTELs, it would mean that to make educators care about this population of students the focus must be on how they have been harmed through the educational system in order to create motivation to fix the system. The title of the seminal text that funneled much of the attention to the LTEL students in California and nationwide referenced this theory of change explicitly in its title: *Reparable Harm* (Olsen, 2010). While focusing on harm to create a motivation for change seems to be a good strategy because it appears to move from a focus on individuals to the context, Tuck emphasizes that damage-centered research is susceptible to a "pathologizing analysis" of individuals and communities that pushes the social and historical context to the periphery. Indeed, this is what has happened in the way in which LTEL students themselves have been represented within damage-centered narratives that are aimed at educators and other education professionals. As described above, bilingual students become LTELs who are characterized by deficits in both languages.

Damage-centered research can create a forum for change. It has engendered a language to differentiate between students like Santiago (the teenage boy whose story began this chapter) and a student who is classified as an EL and new to the English language. In addition, the previously referenced *Reparable Harm* publication was fundamental in the State of California creating the *long-term English language learner* and *at-risk to become LTELL* designation (Maxwell, 2012). The LTEL designation has been cited in numerous newspaper articles, policy documents, and research studies to call attention to the ways in which LTELs are distinct from other adolescent EL populations (e.g., Gerson, 2016; Watanabe, 2014; U.S. Department of Education, 2016). Nevertheless, it is important to recognize the negative consequences for the individuals and communities that are at the center of educational reform that is motivated by damage-centered narratives. Specifically, it is necessary to talk about the consequences of the LTEL label and associated views about students.

Power of Labels

García (2009) illustrates how the language used to identify bilingual young people impacts multiple aspects of their educational experiences. For instance, she notes how referring to students as *emergent bilinguals* rather than *limited English proficient* or *English language learners* highlights their potential, rather than a lack. In addition, she notes that this framing provides a way for educators to build upon students' strengths, namely their home language and cultural practices (p. 323). In this way, labels and associated views about students are powerful. This power of labels is not unique to those that describe students' linguistic backgrounds. Educational research highlights similar phenomena with other terms such as *struggling reader* (Alvermann, 2006; Frankel & Brooks, 2018), *at-risk* (Brown, 2016), and *urban* (Milner, 2012).

In looking specifically at the predominant linguistic and literate abilities that are ascribed to students identified as long-term English learners, researchers have highlighted a number of dangers of this current framing. For example, the LTEL label places the focus on English in a way that renders invisible other factors that influence a student's educational experiences. These other factors include students' racial/ethnic background (Flores & Rosa, 2015), their previous literacy instructional experiences (Brooks, 2015), and the complexities of their everyday literacy practices (de los Ríos, 2018). It is for this reason that researchers like Menken and Kleyn, who initially contributed to this framing of students in their early work, have specifically reformulated the way in which they talk about the population of students who are considered to be long-term English learners (Flores et al., 2015; Menken, 2013).

The conversation about labels is about more than just words. Labels impact the way in which educators engage with students and understand their needs and abilities (Hernandez, 2017; Protacio & Jang, 2016; Salerno & Kibler, 2016). The focus on limited English literacy abilities that is generated by LTEL label and predominant coinciding descriptions means that possible educational approaches to this population are frequently constrained around "fixing" students' English abilities (Kibler & Valdés, 2016; Kleyn & Stern, 2018). For instance, I have witnessed LTELs being placed for many years in the same computerized reading intervention program in order to build up their English reading abilities, which were seen as nonexistent. These types of educational approaches constrain teachers' abilities to engage in collaborative teaching and learning with their students. Moreover, it makes it even more difficult to implement teaching and learning that engages with the social realities that impact students' lives.

Humanizing Reading Instruction for LTELs

I was motivated to write this book as a response to the damage-centered narratives that are predominant among practitioner-oriented texts. This book rejects dehumanizing instructional practices that frame students who are considered to be LTELs as deficient. It is for this reason that this book challenges the commonplace descriptions of LTELs that have found popularity in the media and teacher-focused publications. This book tackles reading in English because it plays an important role in the educational lives of adolescents across the secondary curriculum in the United States and other countries and contexts where English is the medium of instruction (Alvermann, 2001; Bunch, Walqui, & Pearson, 2014; Lee & Spratley, 2010). Reading is not limited to one content area; it plays an principal role across the curriculum. Reading is key even in disciplines that can be viewed as solely numerical, like math (Avalos, Zisselsberger, Langer-Osuna, & Secada, 2015; Czocher & Maldonado, 2015; Mosqueda, Bravo, Solís, Maldonado, & De La Rosa, 2016). Moreover, adults' judgments about whether or not adolescents are successful readers can impact the courses to which they have access in school (Gomez, 2004; Frankel, 2016; Learned, 2016) and whether or not they are considered to be proficient in English (King & Bigelow, 2016; Reyes & Domina, 2019; Schissel & Kangas, 2018).

For some, the idea of dehumanizing pedagogical practices in the context of everyday schooling and literacy learning of high school students may seem extreme; therefore, it is important to understand what is meant by this term. Drawing on the work of Freire (1984) and other scholars (e.g., Balderrama, 2001; Burke et al., 2008) who built upon his philosophical offerings, del Carmen Salazar (2013, p. 127) illustrates how pedagogy can be dehumanizing. She writes: "Teachers and students are devalued and dehumanized through mechanical pedagogical approaches that distract them from meaningful learning and silence their collective voices." In addition, Irizarry and Brown (2014) discuss how dehumanizing pedagogical practices are more frequently engaged in with students who are the target of programs to rectify "achievement gaps." This book is written from a frame that pushes against the dehumanizing schooling experiences that many students who are considered LTELs encounter.

Qualitative research about secondary students provides insight into the consequences of dehumanizing pedagogical practices because it provides a space for students when their voices are typically unheard (Bertrand, Durand, & Gonzalez, 2017; Nyachae, 2019). For instance, Learned (2016) shows how students who were identified as struggling readers reported more frequently than their non-struggling reader counterparts that their voices were not valued in school. Armando, a student in Flores et al.'s (2015) study of LTELs, shares the consequences of the dehumanizing schooling practice of repeatedly assessing proficiency in what a young person considers to be their primary language:

Armando: So seven times in a row, seven years in a row?
Interviewer: So … yeah. If you don't pass the exam, then you stay a [long-term] English learner.
Armando: You made me feel stupid.

Flores et al., 2015, p. 113

Again, the voice of Armando as someone who identifies as an English-speaker is ignored by the repeated assessment and his following failure to be institutionally identified as an English speaker. The consequences of a dehumanizing instructional experiences are that students' multidimensional identities and abilities are flattened, and young people are rendered "less than human."

Instruction that challenges damage-centered narratives about this student population must begin by challenging the LTEL label. It does this by resisting frequently voiced perspectives that characterize students who are considered to be LTELs by their supposed deficits in language, literacy, and education. It is this rejection of damage and deficiency that is fundamental to instructional approaches that have been put forth to challenge the dehumanizing pedagogical practices that have been characteristic of the schooling for minoritized students (e.g., Culturally Responsive Pedagogy [Ladson-Billings, 1995, 2014]; Culturally Sustaining Pedagogy [Paris, 2012; Paris & Alim, 2014]). However, engaging in humanizing pedagogy requires more than rejection of deficiency. It requires the creation of an affirming and supportive environment in which learning can take place (Edwards, MacArthur, & Russell-Owens, 2016; Joseph, Hailu, & Matthews, 2019; Rosario-Ramos, 2018). With these goals in mind, this book provides multiple pathways for educators of LTELs to engage in a multifaceted lens of reading education. To draw on the words of Golden and Womack (2016), "The goal is not to 'fix' those labeled 'struggling,' 'disruptive,' or 'at risk' but to shift the contexts that position learners in these ways, including our own practices and relationships with the adolescents with whom we teach and learn" (p. 41).

LTELs, Literacy Instruction, and the Importance of Framing

A first step towards engaging in literacy instruction that is not centered in perceived shortcomings of students and resists dehumanizing practices is to dissect the LTEL label. One tool towards this goal is to recognize that all labels, as Kibler and Valdés (2016) illustrate, that are applied to language learners are manufactured. Through analyzing labels, which have been used over the course of one hundred years, they highlight how descriptions of language learners are not as neutral as they appear. In this context of being manufactured, they identify the how language learner labels rely on particular ideas about language, particular curricular organizations, and particular ideas about the ways in which languages are learned. These understandings are not value-free but draw on particular theoretical traditions and ways of interpreting the world. For the purposes of day-to-day literacy education, I argue that this recognition of the manufacturing of language learner labels means that how educators respond to them is not fixed. As labels are manufactured, educators have the power to re-envision the way in which they are used and operate in their classroom.

In saying that educators can re-envision how labels operate in their classroom, I mean that the way in which the label is used as a part of instruction and interpreted is in the hands of educator. For example, del Carmen Salazar and Fránquiz (2008) describe the pedagogical practices of a high school ESL teacher whose name was Ms. Corazón. Ms. Corazón worked within a department in which student input into the curriculum was shunned. However, del Carmen Salazar and Fránquiz (2008, p. 188) documented how she was able to create a more humanizing environment by using what they refer to as a "picture walk" through the ESL textbook to identify topics about which the students wanted to learn. The students selected civil rights. Through this topic choice, Ms. Corazón was able to incorporate student voices, the textbook, and explicit instruction on genres (e.g., biography), so students were able to make key connections with their own background knowledge. In a more recent study, Ascenzi-Moreno (2017) examines how an English as a New Language teacher, Karla, demonstrated her understanding of her recently arrive student's oral and literate abilities in English and Haitian-Creole when she created a context for the student to write the first draft of an autobiographical assignment in Haitian-Creole. These educators' practices did not combat the larger processes in the way in which bilingual students were positioned in schools or society. Moreover, they were limited by various restrictions at the school level. Nevertheless, they used the power within their classrooms to create a different kind of learning environment for their students. Even when forced to work within contexts in which specific labels carry weight, educators have the power to envision distinct ways of recognizing who their students are and what they can do (Menken & García, 2010).

Now, this reframing of the way in which educators understand students who are considered to be LTELs is not about making magical visions of students that are not based in reality. It is about the power of alternative frames to make discernible what has been rendered invisible by the predominant way of seeing. This re-envisioning requires another way to conceive of this population of students who have come to be called long-term English learners.

Alternative Frames for Understanding LTEL Student Experiences

The first thing that is essential to know about the LTEL label is that it is the product of a specific set of educational policies. As a result, it is not a definitive description of students' linguistic abilities. Therefore, it is necessary to learn about the students who become classified as LTELs and why they remain in the EL classification. Students are triggered to be initially tested for their English language proficiency because of a home language survey, which seeks to identify the primary language used in the home. Although this home language survey may accurately identify students, it is important to recognize that—depending on its construction and caregivers' understanding of the question—it may over- or under-identify students as possible ELs (Goldenberg & Rutherford-Quach, 2012; Zehr, 2010). Following this initial identification via the home language survey, the next step is to assess students' English language proficiency. Students' performance in this initial assessment will determine if they are classified as ELs. If students are classified as ELs, their English proficiency is evaluated annually until they meet the exit/reclassification criteria (see Figure 1.2).

Many states in the United States belong to consortia that use a particular English language proficiency assessment (e.g., WIDA, ELPA21). The State of Illinois, which is part of the WIDA consortium, requires specific scores on ACCESS for ELLs to determine whether an EL is eligible for exit. Specifically, they provide a score for overall composite proficiency that integrates reading, writing, speaking, and listening. Other states, which are not part of these consortia, have their own state-designed English language proficiency assessments and requirements. For example, in Texas the TELPAS is used for accountability purposes. However, the assessments that are used for the exit criteria for middle school and high school can vary. They must include students' performance on approved assessments of oral English language proficiency. Then, reading and writing scores are determined from either state standardized achievement tests or another approved assessment of literacy. In addition, teachers' subjective evaluations also play a role in this assessment process.

As educators who are working with students who are classified as long-term English learners, it can be unclear as to why understanding this entire process is fundamental to working with the population of students. As I mentioned above, the recognition that the LTEL label is not a description of linguistic and literate abilities, but a product of specific implementation of policy is a reminder that the labels that are applied to middle and high school students are not exact and neutral descriptions (Brooks, 2017; Kibler & Valdés, 2016; Thompson, 2015). They are the product of a process that is influenced by the actions of individuals, beliefs about language, particular ideas about language and language learning that

In this chapter, I have discussed general criteria for how a student's English language proficiency is determined within particular states. However, these criteria can vary by state, district, and even school. Find the exit criteria required for students to move from being classified as ELs to being considered proficient in English in your district. Some good places to find information include: your school or district's website, the EL specialist/administrator, or local professional organizations related to EL education. After you find this information, consider the following questions:

• Were the criteria different than you imagined?

• If you could add/remove aspects of the criteria what would you change?

FIGURE 1.2 Digging deeper: What are your district's EL reclassification criteria?

are taken by research, and interpretations of policy requirements. For example, the LTEL label highlights that from the time that students are very young, literacy practices that are associated with reading and writing in particular ways are considered English proficiency for bilingual students. This process is distinct from those who are considered monolingual English speakers because regardless of how well students are doing in the language of schooling it does not impact whether or not they are considered proficient in English. It highlights that there are two standards of English proficiency institutionalized into the school system: one for monolinguals[3] and one for bilinguals. As a result, the way in which students are currently identified is only one of many possibilities of the way their linguistic abilities could be understood.

Acknowledging that the labels that are applied to students' linguistic abilities are not definitive descriptions of their linguistic abilities encourages educators to ask different questions about the linguistic backgrounds of the LTELs who are in their classrooms. Specifically, educators can see the identification of English learners as a bureaucratic process that is based on a certain set of assumptions about who students are and what English proficiency is, which does not necessarily accurately describe a student's abilities. As a result, this conceptualization of language labels requires asking: For what bureaucratic reasons are students remaining in the EL classification (Brooks, 2018)? This question is critical because it reinforces that a classification is not a description of linguistic ability. It is the result of a specific policy process. Therefore, understanding how students come to be in particular policy categories is important to being able to create classroom environments that are supportive of this student population. For example, identifying whether a student remains classified as an EL because of a math grade or because of their performance on an oral language proficiency assessment can provide insight into this student's experience on the official level (see Figure 1.3).

Interpretations of LTELs' Reading Practices. LTEL is not merely a neutral description of the length of a student's classification as an English learner. In the context of literacy instruction, the normative LTEL lens obscures what this population of adolescent bilinguals is able to do with literacy, their experiences with

If you have students who are considered to be LTELs in your classroom, explore why two or three have remained ELs. This requires looking up their educational history. In addition to identifying when students began schooling in the U.S. and their official home language, the remaining information that you should collect depends on the criteria for being considered proficient in English. Other interesting information to learn could also include how many schools the student has attended and what type of language programming they received (bilingual education, ESL, etc.). After this information has been collected, consider the following questions:

• What did you notice about these students' educational histories?

• Did anything surprise you?

• How can you incorporate this information into your instructional routine?

• Consider petitioning for this type of analysis to be done within your department or grade-level.

FIGURE 1.3 Digging deeper: Understanding ongoing classification as an EL

literacy, and the nature of their literacy difficulties. The predominant framing of the LTEL label marginalizes many young people's sophisticated use of English and erases other relevant aspects of their identities and experiences.

Returning to the student Alexis whose rap songs I described as illustrating his ability to use a variety of literary devices in English. I selected him for this example because he was identified as an LTEL, he was not new to the English language, he was born in the United States, and he had been educated in the United States since kindergarten. One of the main reasons that was classified as an EL was because of his low reading scores on standardized assessments of reading that were used to determine his English proficiency. Through the dominant LTEL lens, his English reading difficulties were evidence that he had yet to learn English.

On the surface, this interpretation of Alexis' reading test scores seems like an appropriate conceptualization of language for an academic context. As Cummins, an oft-cited researcher in questions of language proficiency of bilingual students wrote:

> If children are unable to handle the context-reduced demands of an English test, there is little reason to believe that they have developed sufficient "English proficiency" to compete on an equal basis with native English-speaking children in a regular English classroom.
>
> *Cummins, 1984, p. 16*

However, this conceptualization of the relationship between performance on standardized literacy assessments and English proficiency reflects a simplistic view of literacy. It places English proficiency center stage, and other factors that influence a student's literacy practices are pushed to the periphery.

The interpretation of Alexis' performance on standardized assessment of reading reflects a one-dimensional understanding of literacy. It treats reading as if it was just another part of language proficiency. However, literacy and language are distinct but interrelated. With the exception of those with major developmental difficulties, all human beings acquire language (either spoken or signed). However, the ways of using written language that are recognized as reading proficiency on standardized assessments reflect an individual's experience with formal schooling. Therefore, like Valdés, MacSwan, and Alvarez (2009, p. 9), I contend that literacy is better understood as an aspect of academic achievement rather than language proficiency. They note that the description of literacy as a reflection of academic achievement does not negate the role of language in school-based literacy practices; however, they are not one and the same. Therefore, it is necessary to know more about Alexis' experiences with language, literacy, and schooling before determining whether his test scores are attributable to his English proficiency or some other factors.

What other factors are important in reading academic texts? From multiple theoretical perspectives on reading, it is understood that more than the ability to comprehend language is necessary to construct meaning with texts (e.g., de la Piedra, 2011; Lewis, Enciso, & Moje, 2007; Hull & Moje, 2012 Smagorinsky, 2001a; Sturtevant et al., 2006). Snow and Biancarosa (2003), drawing on the RAND Reading Group's review of the literature on reading comprehension, identify more than 50 factors that influence how an individual reads. Their chart illustrates that competencies associated with language play a role in comprehension (e.g., oral language ability, linguistic knowledge, and general vocabulary). However, there are many factors beyond language that influence meaning-making with texts, such as identity as a reader, domain-specific knowledge, and school quality. More recent reviews of the literature (e.g., Franzak, 2006; Lee & Spratley, 2010; Lesaux & Geva, 2006; Phelps, 2005) identify similar factors as being relevant to understanding how individuals read as those found by the RAND Reading Study Group. The relevance of these multiple factors should not minimize the fact that for some students classified as ELs, their newness to the English language may mean that language-related difficulties play a larger role. However, when instructing bilingual or multilingual readers, the reliance on English proficiency to explain reasons for difficulty must be examined. It is important to ensure that educators investigate the nature of students' difficulties because it provides a pathway for how to build upon students' existing knowledge bases.

More than English Learners: Pushing Past Policy Classifications

In the previous section, I argued that LTEL is a harmful interpretive lens for literacy teaching because it overlooks the complexity of reading. As such, it permits the exclusive attribution, without further investigation, of standardized reading test scores to students' English proficiency. I offered an alternative way of conceptualizing reading that recognizes that reading entails more than knowing a language. If reading entails more than language proficiency, then educators who work with students who remain classified as ELs need a multifaceted conception of literacy and the students with whom they work. The focus on understanding students' linguistic experiences and literacy learning history is illustrative of the literacy as social practice perspective lens that guides research and pedagogical strategies within this book. Rather than an individual cognitive endeavor, this perspective highlights the social nature of literacy (e.g., Barton & Hamilton, 2000; Street, 1984, 2012).

The term *social* is applicable on multiple levels within this perspective. Through this analytic lens, literacy learning is viewed as social because an individual doesn't acquire the various practices associated with "literacy" on his or her own. S/he learns to engage in particular ways of producing and comprehending texts through interactions with others. Second, literacy is social in that it varies according to the sociopolitical context. For example, university freshman frequently learn that what is recognized as successful written communication in college may be distinct from what was valued in their high school English language arts courses. Finally, literacy is social in that the various power dynamics that influence social life also influence which literacy practices are recognized as appropriate in particular contexts. In other words, literacy is not neutral. When literacy is understood as social practice, not only are the multiple knowledges that are necessary to make meaning recognized, but also multiple ways in which people can engage in meaning-making are highlighted.

The conception of literacy as a social practice is vital for literacy pedagogy because it highlights that literacy learning does not take place within a vacuum. The various social identities of learners, teachers, and others engaged in literacy education are also important (Bryan, 2016; Chaparro, 2014; Kinloch, Burkhard, & Penn, 2017; Zapata & Laman, 2016). For example, educators' beliefs about racial groups or the ways in which language is learned impacts learning and teaching (Escamilla, 2006; García-Sánchez, 2016; Everett, 2016; Martínez, Hikida, & Durán, 2015). As a result, this book is centered in a framework that seeks to humanize reading instruction for English-speaking bilinguals who are identified as (long-term) English learners. In the context of an educational environment that emphasizes decontextualized "best practices," this type of pedagogy rejects the underlying philosophy that literacy instruction is about matching the correct method to the appropriate student. As Bartolomé writes:

> The actual strengths of methods depend, first and foremost, on the degree to which they embrace a humanizing pedagogy that values the students' background knowledge, culture, and life experiences, and creates learning contexts where power is shared by students and teachers.
>
> *1994, p. 190*

Humanizing reading instruction requires an in-depth understanding of the students who are considered to be long-term English learners.

A More Humanizing Perspective on Reading Pedagogy

The next four chapters focus on the experiences of five adolescent Latinas who had been classified as English learners since kindergarten: Destiny, Eliza, Lizbeth, Jamilet, and Valeria. At the time of the study, these five teenagers attended New Millennium High School in Southern California. New Millennium High School had approximately 600 students enrolled. Demographically, New Millennium High School was similar to their elementary and middle schools. Ninety-five percent of the students identified themselves as Latino, whereas the other 5% is considered to be Black; 97% of the students received free or reduced-fee lunches. Many of the students were the first generation in their family to be born in the United States; their parents originated from Mexico, El Salvador, Guatemala, and Belize. However, the majority of the students themselves were born in Southern California, or they had arrived early in elementary school. The school had a very small population of recent immigrant students. Almost 30% of the student body was classified as ELs with a "primary language" of Spanish. Many of the students who were not currently classified as ELs had been classified as ELs at some point in their educational path.

I selected these particular five female students after administering a sociolinguistic survey about student language use, which I distributed to the entire tenth-grade class during various periods of their Spanish class. The survey inquired about how the students used their languages at home, school, and in other social spaces. Based on the survey, I identified those students who had been classified as ELs for at least seven years prior to high school and reported that they spoke English on a daily basis. Then, I decided to only use female participants because maintaining same-gender relationships made my research more socially acceptable in this community. The final consideration in identifying participants was their class schedule, because I planned to observe students in clusters in their sophomore biology and English language arts classes. Destiny, Eliza, Jamilet, Lizbeth, and Valeria were the teenagers who met the requisite criteria and from whom I was able to obtain parental consent and student assent to participate in the research.

This book's primary contribution to educators is a detailed analysis of literacy learning as it is instantiated in the lives of five young women who are part of a growing, yet under-researched demographic of adolescent students. However, it goes one step further to highlight practical ways in which educators can enact humanizing reading pedagogy that is informed by social perspectives of reading and bilingualism. This book represents an interconnection between research and practice. As such, each chapter reflects a different level of focus on these five students and their classroom experiences. The second chapter uses the focal students' lives as a forum to explore significant issues relating to bilingualism, and presents an alternative conception of the language backgrounds of LTELs.

Chapters 3 and 4 move away from the focus on individual students and foreground the examination of the textual environment and dominant classroom meaning-making practices of their biology and English language arts classroom. These patterns are contextualized in the broader patterns of their educational histories. Chapter 5 returns to a focus on individual students to provide an analysis of their reading practices that are contextualized in their classroom experiences of reading. Finally, Chapter 6 brings together the chapters in a concrete way that reflects the lessons learned throughout the book.

Significance of this Book

Instead of focusing on students' individual "failure" to learn English, this book builds on the scholarship of other researchers whose work focuses on bilingual students' *opportunity to learn* (Bartlett, 2007; Callahan, 2005; Escamilla, 2015; Valdés, 2001). Opportunity to learn is a term that can have multiple meanings. On the most superficial level, some take it to mean mere exposure to particular content. However, when I use this term I draw on the tradition of research that asserts a more robust theory of learning. For the purposes of this book, I highlight one of Gee's (2003, p. 31) six principals as it relates to the conceptualizing opportunity to learn with regard to reading assessments. He writes:

> People (children or adults) have not had the same opportunity to learn based solely on how much or how little they have read "in general," but in terms of how equivalent their experience has been with reading specific types of text in specific sorts of ways. They must have also had equivalent experience with the social practices associated with reading these specific types of texts in these specific ways. Finally, they must have had equivalent experiences in being producers and not just consumers of texts of that type read in that way.

Rather than assuming that students who are considered to be LTELs are experiencing difficulties with literacy because of their "limited English proficiency," this book pushes educators to be aware of their students' previous opportunities to learn desired reading practices, existing reading practices, and the ongoing opportunities to learn that they create in their own classrooms. As a result, this book highlights the significance of students' experiences with literacy learning and the power of appropriate literacy pedagogy that recognizes students' existing abilities and engages them in authentic literacy practices that can provide pathways to diverse post-secondary educational and career opportunities.

Notes

1 All identifying names are pseudonyms.
2 Certain definitions, like the one institutionalized by the State of California, include additional criteria (e.g., performance on standardized assessments). However, requirements that extend beyond the number of years of classification are uncommon in research and practice.
3 In my exploration of Home Language Surveys, several states identify World Englishes, which are varieties of English that do not have their origins in the United States of America, Canada, the United Kingdom, Australia, or New Zealand (e.g., Nigerian English, Indian English, Singaporean English). Motha (2014) also documents the practice of students who are speakers of World English being placed in ESL. As a result, not all monolingual English speakers may be treated as such. World English speakers may be assessed in ways that mirrors those who are new to the English language.

2

BILINGUALISM AND STUDENTS WHO ARE LABELED LTELS

I can speak Spanish. I just get nervous.

Eliza Stone

During my first interaction with Eliza Stone, her white skin, green eyes, and dyed red hair became central to the discussion of language in her tenth-grade "Spanish for Native Speakers" class. The teacher, Ms. Alvarado, had explained instructions for the first assignment using Spanish. Eliza raised her hand and asked for clarification in English, a language practice that she frequently engaged in at home. As Eliza shared with me later, she was asking for clarification about the nature of the assignment. However, Ms. Alvarado switched from Spanish to English to answer Eliza's question. She thought that Eliza could not understand Spanish. In response to Ms. Alvarado's language shift, another student laughed and said, "She thinks you're a White girl." Most of the class began to laugh. Eliza defended herself by explaining, "I can speak Spanish. I just get nervous."

Eliza asked the question in English not realizing that it would facilitate Ms. Alvarado thinking that she did not know Spanish. Eliza was accustomed to addressing Spanish-speaking adults in English with the assumption that they would continue to respond to her in Spanish. In Eliza's home the linguistic rule that was followed was that everyone spoke the language that was most comfortable for them (if they knew that their conversation partner understood). Eliza, like many other students who are considered to be long-term English learners, felt more comfortable speaking English (Brooks, 2017; Menken & Kleyn, 2010). Therefore, she asked a question in this language. Different linguistic communication norms as well as the way in which Eliza was perceived racially contributed to this classroom interaction.

I begin this chapter by describing Eliza's experience because it illustrates key themes that undergird this chapter. Specifically, it highlights the interconnection of perceptions of language proficiency, race, and linguistic ability. Moreover, it illustrates how linguistic identities are not always what they seem to be. Eliza understood her Spanish teacher, but chose to use another language because of her own linguistic insecurities. This individual choice because of how she looked sent a different message to the teacher and her classmates about what she could do with Spanish.

This chapter, which begins with an interaction that highlights the misinterpretation of linguistic abilities, continues the work of the previous chapter of moving reading instruction beyond static classifications such as *long-term English learner*. Instruction should begin with a nuanced understanding of students' complex linguistic experiences. Recognizing this complexity is important because it illustrates that students are not solely long-term learners of English but bilinguals with a multifaceted linguistic expertise—whether or not this linguistic expertise is registered by their performance on standardized assessments. This type of recognition is imperative because it provides a base for teachers to "support young people in sustaining the cultural and linguistic competence of their communities while simultaneously offering access to dominant cultural competence" (Paris, 2012, p. 95). This approach rejects the lens of deficiency that is common to the description of students who are considered to be LTELs. Therefore, this chapter presents an alternative conception of the bilingualism of LTELs. This conception and resulting student-focused descriptions set the stage for the remaining chapters that examine their English language reading practices and provide pathways for educators to create opportunities to learn within their classrooms.

Valuing the Devalued

In the previous chapter, I argued that creating more humanizing literacy instruction means not using the LTEL label as a guide for teaching. The LTEL label makes it hard for literacy educators to know students on the deeper level that is necessary to base instruction on students' existing abilities and experiences. The static linguistic descriptions that are attached to the LTEL label may appear as if teaching is being informed by students' background knowledge, culture, and life experiences. For example, the LTEL label allows for differentiation from other types of adolescent students who are classified as ELs, like recently arrived refugee students or a high school student who chooses to "study abroad" for a year. As a result, teaching to the LTEL label can be seen as a way of affirming U.S.-educated students' identities and backgrounds as distinct. However, researchers have noted that misguided attempts to draw on students' culture and linguistic practices in the name of culturally responsive instruction can contribute to a static representation of students' linguistic abilities (Ladson-Billings, 2014; Paris, 2012; Paris & Alim,

Examine the walls of your classroom. Are languages other than English represented? Including representations of the linguistic practices of the students in your classroom, the people in the school community, and people in other parts of the world is an easy way to signal to students that linguistic diversity is welcome. Be sure to show students that academic work can be accomplished in more than just English. Languages other than English should not only be relegated to holiday celebrations.

FIGURE 2.1 Create change: Linguistic environment update

2014). In other words, educators teach to stereotypes of what students are. An added problem for students considered to be LTELs is that the way in which linguistic descriptions are articulated are situated in discourses of deficiency (Flores et al., 2015; Rosa, 2016). These static representations offer misleading insight into students' abilities and experiences.

Rather than the LTEL label, it is more pedagogically enriching for educators to use bilingualism as a frame to understand LTELs' linguistic backgrounds. In this section, I highlight characteristics about bilingualism that are essential for educators of LTELs to appreciate. Notably, this conception of bilingualism challenges commonly held myths about bilingualism. As a result, it provides a framework that looks beyond what traditional English literacy instruction for bilinguals may entail. Then, I use these ideas about bilingualism to describe the linguistic experiences of the five teenagers who are the focal students of this research. I decided to lay out this framework using the five girls on whom this book focuses to show what this alternative framing means for understanding the linguistic lives of students who are considered to be LTELs.

Bilingualism for English Reading Pedagogy

On the surface, it may seem self-evident as to what individuals mean when they use terms such as *bilingual* or *multilingual*. However, it is not as simple as it appears. An instructional activity that I use with pre-service teachers in my classes demonstrates the trickiness of defining bilingualism. I ask pre-service teachers to define bilingualism independently and share their definitions with the entire class. Through this process of individual reflection and sharing, it becomes evident that there are varying definitions of what bilingual means. For instance, some people write about the ability to communicate in two languages orally; others include reading and writing in both languages; still others put qualifications like "perfectly," and other talk about feeling comfortable within bilingual communities. While there are certain aspects of bilingualism that pre-service teachers may gather in common, there is not one singular definition of bilingualism that is held across any class.

These varying descriptions about bilingualism are not unique to people who are new to academically learning about the topic. For instance, Chin &

Wigglesworth (2007) discuss five ways in which bilingualism is described within research. Specifically, they identify descriptors that refer to the degree of bilingualism (i.e., a specific level of proficiency), those that refer to the contexts in which bilinguals acquired their languages (i.e., at school or amongst family), the age at which individuals learn their languages (i.e., childhood or adult bilingual), the domains of use (i.e., schooling or religious purposes), and the relationship of bilingual to the social context (i.e., bilingual raised in a primarily monolingual society versus a bilingual raised in a multilingual society). These are not the only ways that bilingualism can be described. However, they illustrate that even within the research literature bilingualism is a permeable concept.

Educators of adolescents tend to receive limited information about students' bilingualism. It is often restricted to the results of English language proficiency assessments that reveal little about students' knowledge of languages other than English or how they use their languages on a daily basis. Moreover, they only provide a snapshot into one particular way of envisioning students' English language abilities. As Rosa (2019) notes, the focus on limited English proficiency and an absence of discussion of any other linguistic abilities often positions students who are bilingual and labeled as ELs as having no linguistic abilities.

If educators look deeply into students' files, information from their home language survey and initial identification as an EL might be available. It could show that perhaps they entered schools as bilinguals (but did not pass the English proficiency test) or that they learned English while in school. When students are LTELs, this information from the initial identification and home language survey is often more than ten years old. As a result, it is likely that the linguistic lives of students have changed. Lam's (2009) research with a recent immigrant from Shanghai, China shows how bilingual language use can shift over a short period of time. The focal student of the study, Kaiyee, described herself as arriving in the United States feeling equally comfortable speaking Shanghainese and Mandarin. However, her linguistic situation changed when her peer group evolved to include other Chinese immigrant adolescents whose primary language was Cantonese, but could also speak Mandarin. As a result of this change in her peer group and her increased use of Mandarin, she described herself as becoming more proficient in Mandarin since immigrating to the United States. Moreover, over the course of the eight-month analysis of the study Lam found that Kaiyee was drawing on features of various types of Englishes and still expanding her ways of using Shanghainese. These changes happened within the life of a recent immigrant over a relatively short span of time, for students who are considered to be long-term English learners these types of changes can happen over the course of more than a decade. Therefore, initial descriptions of primary languages of the home might not be accurate.

Other than the results of the home language survey, other aspects about students' bilingualism (e.g., students' relationship with their home languages and communities) are not easily accessible to educators. Certain educators who teach within bilingual programs may have access to this information; however, bilingual programs at the secondary level are far less common (Gándara & Escamilla, 2017). Yet, this kind of information is fundamentally necessary to be able to engage in the kind of humanizing instruction that recognizes the linguistic abilities that students bring to school. The following conception of bilingualism can help educators identify and learn about the aspects of their students' linguistic lives that are not within the cumulative records of LTELs.

Language Use and Dynamic Bilingualism

First, I draw on Grosjean's (2008) conceptualization of bilinguals to identify the five girls on whom this book focuses as bilinguals. Grosjean writes that bilinguals are "those people who use two or more languages (or dialects) in their everyday lives" (p. 10). As I interpret Grosjean's use of *everyday*, it does not require that an individual actually speak, listen, read, or write in two languages on daily basis. I interpret *everyday* as a synonym for "routinely" or "typically." Specifically, I situate this conceptualization of who is bilingual within the understanding that among socially oriented theories of second-language acquisition that "language is learned through experience and use" (Valdés, Poza, & Brooks, 2015, p. 62). This focus recognizes that the languages an individual uses reflects their linguistic experiences not their specific national, ethnic, or racial identity. For instance, while nationality and language are often seen as interconnected, this view is an artifact of historical processes that valued this type of representation (Flores, 2013; Makoni & Pennycook, 2007; McNamara, Khan, & Frost, 2015). The reality of linguistic diversity in various nation-states is quite different. For educators, knowledge about students' linguistic experiences is fundamental to being able to build on their linguistic strengths in the service of literacy education.

In addition to the conceptualization that bilinguals are those individuals who use two or more languages in their everyday lives, I draw on García's (2009) conception of dynamic bilingualism to frame how I understand the way in which a bilingual's individual language is organized within their mind. Rather than envisioning bilinguals' languages as two independent systems or some other configuration, dynamic bilingualism puts forth the idea that bilinguals have "one linguistic system that has features that more often practiced according to societally constructed and controlled 'languages,' but other times producing new practices" (García & Wei, 2014, p. 16). For students who are considered to be long-term English learners, this would "mean not treating them as speakers of their home language(s) and English but rather as legitimate users of fluid language forms that reflect the dynamic nature of the communities that they come from" (Flores, 2013, p. 283). Instead of seeking to understand bilinguals through a monolingual viewpoint, Flores argues for the importance of appreciating bilinguals' linguistic abilities within bilingual linguistic norms.

This conception of bilingualism does not value the achievement of the mythical "balanced bilingual" who has mirrored abilities in both languages. The bilingual person who has a need to use both languages in the same way in the same context is very rare. Therefore, the expectation that a bilingual has mirrored abilities in both languages is not an accurate description of bilingual life for the overwhelming majority of people. As Valdés (2017) describes:

> Rather than "ideal" bilinguals and "ambilinguals", researchers now argue that bilingual individuals will not be "perfect" (read: monolingual) users of two languages, but simply persons who use resources from two languages in their daily lives for a variety of purposes.

In order to understand how bilingual students use their linguistic resources, educators must be familiar with general concepts about language variation and translanguaging.

Language Variation. The linguistic features upon which bilinguals draw to communicate may not be those that are identified as the "standard" version of a language. In general, the standard variety of language is that which is associated with the written version of a language and the ways in which socially powerful groups speak. However, Lippi-Green (2012) underscores that the notion of a singular standard variety of a language is a myth. It ignores the fact that what receives the name "language" is the reflection of particular sociocultural and historical circumstances (e.g., Makoni & Pennycook, 2007). In education, language variation among monolinguals who are identified as "native speakers" of a language is frequently rendered invisible when they are compared with bilinguals. It is often presumed that all monolinguals speak the "standard" variety of a language.

Those ways of using language that are stigmatized are not frequently given the term *language*. Instead, they are often referred to as *non-standard varieties*, *non-standard dialects*, or to use a term in a linguistically inaccurate manner, *slang*. Although these ways of using language are stigmatized, they are not linguistically inferior (see Figure 2.2 for an exploration of English language variation). These views of supposed linguistic inferiority reflect the negative social beliefs about the people who are thought to use language in these ways (Baker-Bell, 2017; Lippi-Green, 2012; Smith, 2019; Young, 2009). They represent prejudiced views about people who live in former colonies, racially denigrated people, and/or people of low socioeconomic status. In English, some of these varieties are African American English, Indian English, Chicano English, and Appalachian English.

The recognition of the fact that language varies requires the acknowledgment that students' linguistic repertoires may include ways of using language that are associated with prestige varieties and those that are stigmatized. Students draw on these ways of communicating because the way in which bilinguals use their languages reflects their experiences with those languages (Busch, 2012; Hall, Cheng, & Carlson, 2006). This understanding is particularly important for LTELs whom are what Valdés and Figueroa (1994) refer to as *circumstantial bilinguals*.

While certain ways of using English may be stigmatized in society, it is not because they are linguistically inferior. These beliefs reflect language ideologies. As Barrett (2019) succinctly notes "language ideologies are not based on linguistic facts, but are forms of social prejudice" (p. 17). The English that is associated with stigmatized groups in society is often described as "broken," "bad," or "incorrect." However, the development of these ways of using language are the reflection of particular social and historical circumstances. In drawing on the existing research about African American English, Charity Hudley and Mallinson (2011) note that the roots of African American English are in the history of the resilience of linguistically diverse West Africans, who were enslaved by English-speaking Europeans and White Americans, and the continued linguistic ingenuity of Black people within the United States. Similarly, Chicano English reflects the histories of colonization and strength of Mexican Americans in the United States (Fought, 2003; Santa Ana, 1993). There are many more Englishes in the United States. However, I just use these two as exemplars.

Example of Systematicity

Although the particular linguistic practices that are associated with African American English and Chicano English are often considered deficient, when they are analyzed the ideological base of the description of deficiency is made evident. For example, the use of the aspectual *be* in African American English is often the source of jokes and ridicule of African American English speakers (Rickford & Rickford, 2000).

Green (2002) notes that the aspectual *be* has a unique meaning in that it signifies an iterative action. It is for this reason that this use of *be* is often referred to as *habitual be*. Green notes that the terms *usually* or *always* are generally used within what is often referred to as standard English. Within this context, the statement *Kristina be driving* means that *Kristina is usually driving*. Perhaps, Kristina is a racecar driver who is frequently practicing at the track. Green (2002, p. 48) notes that while the aspectual *be* usually occurs before a verb in the –ing form like in the previous example, it does not always occur in this manner. She provides a number of example to illustrate other possibilities:

During the summer, they go off for two weeks, so her checks **be big.** (Bf, 50s)

"During the summer, they go away for two weeks, so her checks are usually big then"

I **be in my office** by 7:30 (Bf, 40s)

"I am usually in my office by 7:30"

This is just one example of the many features associated with African American English that have a systematic nature to their use.

Similarly, Chicano English is characterized by series of features that are often denigrated as evidence of the English of someone who is just learning the language. However, Santa Ana (1993, p. 15) notes: "Chicano English is an ethnic dialect that children acquire as they acquire English in the barrio or other ethnic social setting during their language acquisition period." Two words with distinct meanings in Chicano English are the use of the word *tell* to mean *ask* and *barely* to mean *just recently* (Fought, 2003). I include the examples that Fought (2003, p. 104) provides below:

FIGURE 2.2 Digging deeper: English language variation

8. *tell,* meaning "ask."

Examples:

*If I tell her to jump up, she'll **tell** me how high.* (Avery, 16)

*She was telling my aunt to **tell** them, you know, what, I mean, what's the reason?* (David, 17)

*It depends on what you **tell** me.* (In response to "Can you answer questions in Spanish?") (Chuck, 17)

9. *barely,* meaning "just recently."

Examples:

*He just **barely** got a job you know back with his father.* (Chuck, 17)

*I just **barely** checked in.* (He has been there only 3 weeks) (Jesus, 16)

*They **barely** graduated from high school.* (Hernan, 47)

A Word of Caution

Since the name of the Englishes that I mentioned above are associated with particular ethnic/racial groups, it is important to remember that "one should never define a language or a speech community based solely on racial classification of its speakers. [It is a] fundamental linguistic principle that a language can never be equated with a specific racial group" (Baugh, 2000, p. 85). Ethnicity/race does not determine how someone uses language, but rather linguistic experiences. For example, Martinez's (2016) research illustrates how both African American and Latino language practices influence the language practices of a Latino youth.

FIGURE 2.2 (Cont.)

Circumstantial bilinguals become bilingual in order to function in the dominant society. As a result, language learning is not limited to formal instructional contexts and their linguistic backgrounds are influenced by those with whom they interact in multiple social contexts. Moreover, it also acknowledges that people who are given the identity of "native-speaker" can often produce language that does not follow the standardized norms. Therefore, in a school setting in which a student who is considered to be an LTEL is required to only draw on linguistic features that are associated with English, it may include those that are associated with "non-standard" varieties of English. Within a schooling context that does not recognize the existence of variation within English, this type of English usage can be interpreted as evidence of lack of English proficiency. For instance, researchers (Motha, 2014; Obeng & Obeng, 2006; Bryan et al., 2019) describe how speakers of World Englishes were placed in English as a Second Language programs. Penfield (1983) and Brooks (2017) documented how the English proficiency of bilingual students can be overlooked when they draw on linguistic features that are associated with stigmatized varieties of English that are indigenous to the United States (e.g., African American English and Chicano English) or engage in misspellings that are not unique to those learning English. For both groups of students, this ignorance of language variation meant that their English language abilities were deemed as not really being English.

Translanguaging. In addition to linguistic features associated within different varieties of one language, bilinguals can bring together linguistic features from what are perceived to be different languages to communicate. When conversation partners are able to freely draw from all of the features in their linguistic repertoire to accomplish a communicative task, this is what Otheguy, García, and Reid (2015) refer to as *translanguaging*. They note that bilinguals (like monolinguals) are not always permitted to use their full linguistic repertoire in communication. So, bilinguals are not always translanguaging. Similarly to the ways that specific linguistic features are stigmatized within a language, translanguaging is often devalued and perceived as evidence of limited language knowledge.

The devaluing of translanguaging is evident in the existence of negative attitudes towards what is frequently referred to as *code-switching*, or the practice of using two or more languages in the same utterance or conversation. For example, Balam and de Prada Pérez (2017) found that adolescents in their study believed that code-switching is "evidence of not knowing any language well" (p. 24). Within a translanguaging frame, the specific term *code-switching* would not be appropriate. This term implies a different relationship between languages than is used within this theoretical frame. However, MacSwan (2017) notes that research on code-switching has been fundamental to fighting deficit perspectives about bilingualism. Therefore, I draw on examples from research on code-switching to illustrate how the "language mixing" that is characteristic of translanguaging is not evidence of linguistic deficiency.

Zentella (1997), in her study of bilingualism among Puerto Rican children in *el bloque* in East Harlem, discusses how there was a belief among many community members that code-switching occurred as a "crutch" because an individual does not have knowledge of a particular word or phrase. However, in her seminal study she demonstrated that code-switching occurred for a number of reasons that extended beyond limited language knowledge.

Among other reasons, Zentella documented that code-switching occurred to choose a language that better reflected the proficiency of the person who was being addressed, to share both direct and indirect quotations, to emphasize a particular statement, and to get the attention of a conversation partner. Zentella used the following statement as an example of a child code-switching for emphasis in the form of a shift to another language to repeat the same or a similar statement: "*No me crees?* You don't believe me." In the following statement, shifting from Spanish to English was a way to indicate a "role shift": "My-*mi nombre es Lourdes.* Now we're going to my sister." More recent research about bilinguals that uses translanguaging and/or code-switching as a lens of analysis illustrates similar and other reasons for drawing on linguistic repertoire in ways that challenge monolingual norms that require language separation (e.g., Durán & Palmer, 2014; Gort, 2012; Gort & Sembiante, 2015; Poza, 2018; Martínez, 2010;

Morales, 2016).This research demonstrates that these practices demonstrate bilingual linguistic expertise, not linguistic deficiency.

The Role of Racial Positioning

Throughout this chapter, I have focused on describing how to conceptualize students' language background and the linguistic practices that are associated with bilingualism. However, Flores and Rosa (2015) assert that the way in which someone's language use is treated is not just about their linguistic practices. They recognize the role of raciolinguistic ideologies in highlighting how the racial positioning of people impacts the interpretation of their linguistic abilities. Specifically, they note how the linguistic practices of racialized speakers are seen as being deficient even when objective linguistic analysis indicates the contrary.This role of raciolinguistic ideologies in shaping who gets to be perceived as linguistically competent is noted through diverse research literatures. For instance, there is an extensive body of research that documents how ideas about race, ethnicity, and nationality influence perceptions of intelligibility and linguistic/literate ability (e.g.,Alim, 2010; Baker-Bell, 2017; Brutt-Griffler & Samimy, 2001; Leung, Harris, & Rampton, 1997; Lo, 2016). For instance, the Black immigrant teacher educators in Smith (2019) describe the way in which their linguistic knowledge and abilities were called into question during teaching in spite of the fact that English was their first language and they had advanced academic degrees in the subject matter.

Racially minoritized people are very conscious of the way in which their racial positioning impacts how they are interpreted by others (e.g., Alvarez, Canagarajah, Lee, Lee, & Rabbi, 2017; Amin, 1997; Faez, 2012). For example, a student in Kinloch's (2005, p. 95) composition classroom, in an open enrollment university in Houston, poignantly articulates the personal and integrated nature of conceptualizations of language and raciolinguistic ideologies:

> I can read and I can write.Tell me how I can use my skills to move ahead in the world without being judged on my accent, my pronunciation of certain words, and on race.You do know that language rights are always tied into race, right?

This student's words reinforce the necessity acknowledging Flores and Rosa's (2015) call for educators to attend to the role of raciolinguistic ideologies in long-term English learners' positioning as deficient speakers in spite of their bilingualism.

The Focal Students

Given this chapter's focus on understanding the linguistic experiences of students who are considered LTELs, I am going to take the previously discussed ideas about bilingualism to describe the linguistic experiences of the five teenagers who are the focal students of this research. However, it is necessary to acknowledge that I was able to gather this information from observations, students' responses to a survey, talking to students about their linguistic experiences, and their official school records. I was able to access this plethora of information because of my position as a researcher. If I was a classroom teacher, the only information that I would have readily have access to is that their original home language survey indicated that Spanish was spoken at home. In addition, I would have known that their most recent English language proficiency and English language arts test scores indicated that they were struggling with English literacy (see Tables 2.1 and 2.2). Given the drastic difference between the information that I had as a researcher and the information to which most teachers have easy access, a critical question to consider is how could the following descriptions be useful in everyday practice?

TABLE 2.1 Performance on California English language development test in ninth grade

Student Name	Overall	Reading	Writing	Listening	Speaking
Destiny	Intermediate	Intermediate	Early Advanced	Intermediate	Intermediate
Eliza	Intermediate	Intermediate	Early Advanced	Intermediate	Early Advanced
Jamilet	Intermediate	Intermediate	Intermediate	Early Intermediate	Early Advanced
Lizbeth	Intermediate	Intermediate	Intermediate	Intermediate	Intermediate
Valeria	Early Intermediate	Beginning	Early Advanced	Early Intermediate	Early Advanced

Note. The CELDT has five possible language proficiency levels: Beginning, Early Intermediate, Intermediate, Early Advanced, and Advanced.

TABLE 2.2 Performance on California Standards Test, English language arts in sixth, seventh, and ninth grade

Student Name	Sixth Grade	Seventh Grade	Ninth Grade
Destiny	Below Basic	Basic	Basic
Eliza	Below Basic	Far Below Basic	Basic
Jamilet	N/A	N/A	Basic
Lizbeth	Far Below Basic	Far Below Basic	Basic
Valeria	Far Below Basic	Far Below Basic	Below Basic

Note. The CST-ELA has five possible achievement levels: Far Below Basic, Below Basic, Basic, Proficient, and Advanced.

The descriptions of the five focal students are important because they shed light on how much information regarding their linguistic experiences and abilities is hidden from official records. It provides a clear vision as to why teachers should learn this kind of information about students. Moreover, there is an easy-to-use survey at the end of the chapter that educators could use to learn similar information about students in a more efficient manner (see Figure 2.4).

Although it is essential to learn from the previously discussed perspectives on bilingual language use and the additional sources of information about Destiny, Eliza, Jamilet, Lizbeth, and Valeria's experiences with Spanish and English, it is crucial to recognize that an individual's experience with and use of language is dynamic. Therefore, the following descriptions are not necessarily an accurate description of their language use at this very moment. Rather, such descriptions reflect how the students described, and I perceived, their language use at the time of this study. Despite these limitations, the following descriptions provide insight into the linguistic background that their "official" representation as (long-term) English learners with a primary language of Spanish ignores.

Five Focal Students' Linguistic Histories

Destiny Lopez. Destiny, like most girls in the tenth grade, had bangs that were parted to the side. They covered most of her forehead, which hid the chicken-pox scar on her otherwise flawless chocolate complexion. Most mornings she used a flatiron to straighten her bangs and braided the rest of her curly hair into a plait that fell over her left shoulder. When she was not around, some of the other students would call her Avatar because she looked similar to Afro-Latina actress Zoe Saldana, who portrayed one of the main characters in the movie *Avatar*. Destiny and her younger brother were the only two in her immediate family to be born in the United States; her parents emigrated from Mexico when her two older siblings were in elementary school. Destiny's parents owned a tamale catering business, and the three younger children lived in a single-family home with their parents. In the high school enrollment paperwork, Destiny's mother described their home as a monolingual Spanish-speaking environment. However, Destiny explained that this situation changed when her older siblings entered U.S. elementary schools. Since that time, the home environment gradually moved towards one in which English was dominant among her siblings, and monolingual Spanish conversations were limited to interactions with adults. It appeared that the home language survey represented the linguistic reality of Destiny's interactions with her mother, rather than Destiny's experience with her siblings or friends.

Outside of the home, Destiny lived in an English-dominant world, but not a monolingual English world. She mostly spoke English with her friends, but she used both languages freely when necessary for her communicative needs. The only time that Destiny had been in a Spanish-dominant linguistic environment outside of the home was when her family returned to Mexico for a year during fifth grade. She explained to me that it was difficult for her to adjust to life back in Mexico:

> It was hard because you'll turn around and they'll talk Spanish, and turn the other way and then Spanish, and if you wanted to say something it was kind of hard to say it in Spanish because you couldn't, like, say it.

After a few months, Destiny stopped going to school in Mexico because learning academic content in Spanish was too challenging. Destiny was accustomed to being in an educational environment in which most of her teachers were monolingual English-speakers, and she could use all of her languages to communicate with the majority of her peer group.

Eliza Stone. At the beginning of the chapter, during my first interaction with Eliza, her white skin, green eyes, and dyed red hair became central to the discussion of language in Spanish class. Eliza's parents were immigrants from El Salvador, who met in Los Angeles. Her parents worked in upscale hotels. Eliza's mother was the head of the laundry department and her father was a car valet. Eliza was very close to her mother, with whom she lived, but had an estranged relationship with her father since he had remarried. Eliza's mother had four children from three different relationships: a 32-year old daughter, a 21-year-old daughter, 16-year-old Eliza, and a son in elementary school. The three youngest children lived in the family home along with Eliza's aunt and her two teenage sons, Eliza's grandmother, Eliza's older sister's African-American boyfriend, and Eliza's mom's Mexican immigrant boyfriend. As a result, a range of language backgrounds was present in Eliza's home—monolingual English speakers, various kinds of bilinguals, and monolingual Spanish speakers.

Unlike other parents, Eliza's father's job required him to interact with English speakers, and he had learned English before she was born. When he lived with Eliza, he would speak to her in English, whereas her mother would speak to her in Spanish. They wanted to ensure that Eliza could speak English before she entered kindergarten. As she progressed through school, she began to use Spanish less frequently. She usually spoke English with her friends, except with her best friend from elementary school, with whom she enjoyed sharing certain Salvadoran Spanish terms. At home, English was the language of choice among young people, but her language use with each adult varied. She usually spoke English with her bilingual aunt and Spanish with her mother. When the topics were too complex for her Spanish abilities, she would have her older sister serve as a translator for conversations with her mother. The only two monolingual Spanish speakers in the home, who had minimal receptive English language abilities, were her grandmother and her mother's boyfriend. Eliza explained that when she did speak with her grandmother, she had no choice but to do so in Spanish and that she rarely interacted with her mother's boyfriend.

On the enrollment paperwork, Eliza's mother described the language history and current linguistic environment differently. She described Eliza as initially a monolingual Spanish-speaking child, who now uses Spanish and English at home, but who was surrounded by monolingual Spanish-speaking adults. Like Destiny, it appears that Eliza's mother's assessment represented her interactions with Eliza as opposed to the totality of Eliza's linguistic experiences. Eliza lived in a bilingual home, but she led a predominantly English life in other social spaces.

Jamilet Lopez. As Jamilet explained to me in one of our first conversations, "Teachers always know my name." Her reputation as a troublemaker, which was highlighted by being expelled from three different middle schools in eighth grade, preceded her everywhere she went. She was a tall, shapely girl, whose dyed black wavy hair stood out against her pale skin and light brown eyes. Jamilet self-identified as being Mexican, but her father was born in Cuba and her mother in El Salvador. Her father had emigrated as a child from Cuba to Mexico and then again from Mexico to the U.S. as an adult. Jamilet's mother arrived in the U.S. from El Salvador as a young adolescent and spoke English to Jamilet when she was a child. However, when Jamilet was ten years old her mother was incarcerated and has had little involvement in Jamilet's life since that time. In the enrollment paperwork that she filled out on behalf of her father, Jamilet indicated that English was her first language as well as being the language that she continues to use most frequently. However, she noted that the adults in her home were Spanish speakers. Jamilet lived in an apartment with her father, who was unemployed; her stepmother, who worked in a local clothing factory; her 30-year-old developmentally disabled stepbrother; and her 20-year-old biological brother. Jamilet's father understood English, but felt most comfortable speaking Spanish. She usually spoke to her father in English and he responded in Spanish. The only monolingual Spanish-speaker in the home, without any English receptive abilities, was her stepmother's son, with whom she did not interact.

Away from home, Jamilet communicated with her friends in English, despite the fact that most of them were English-Spanish bilinguals. She explained to me that she felt more comfortable speaking in English because she is able to express herself better. She felt uncomfortable speaking Spanish because of her Salvadoran accent, her use of what she described as incorrect words, and because her family and friends laughed at her Spanish. Her linguistic environment, inside and outside of the house, allowed her to speak primarily English but also required that she understand Spanish.

Lizbeth Sanchez. "Who?" was the overwhelming response when I asked former teachers and school staff about Lizbeth. Lizbeth blended into the background in her ninth grade year. Her stature might have made it easy for her to become invisible because she was less than five feet tall, with straight long black hair. She had a round brown face with features characteristic of many Mesoamerican Indigenous peoples. She explained to me that she did not talk much in the ninth grade or in middle school. She did not want to call attention to herself because was teased for being short and ugly. Moreover, she noticed that students who were quiet received good grades whether they did the work or not. Nevertheless, this year she did not sit quietly on the periphery. She actively participated in class, asked questions, and made her presence known. As a sophomore, her teachers did not overlook her.

Lizbeth, her twin brother, her 14-year-old sister, and her Chihuahua lived in a one-bedroom apartment with her Mexican-immigrant mother, who worked in a clothing factory. Lizbeth's father returned to Mexico when she was younger, and they were estranged. Lizbeth and her twin brother were the oldest siblings in their family, therefore she was not exposed to English routinely until she entered school. The home language survey on Lizbeth's high school enrollment forms was not completed, so I was not able to access this source of information. However, Lizbeth described her home as being a monolingual Spanish-speaking environment until she entered school. As time passed, Lizbeth's home linguistic environment became a space in which both languages were used interchangeably. She reported that with her siblings she used mostly English, but with her mom she used both Spanish and English. However, her mom only spoke to her in Spanish. Outside of school, Lizbeth used both Spanish and English with her friends. Inside and outside the home, Lizbeth's life required that she use her receptive and productive abilities in both languages.

Valeria Reyes. Unlike most of the other girls in the tenth grade, Valeria wore no make-up. Still, she took great pride in her appearance; her hair was always perfectly styled. She was no more than five feet tall with olive skin and an inviting smile. At the time of the study, her family was experiencing a moment of stability after years of tumult. The current configuration of Valeria's family was the result of her mother's fourth attempt at creating a home. Valeria's mother arrived in South Central Los Angeles, fleeing two failed relationships that forced her to leave three children in Mexico and two children in New York City. In Los Angeles, Valeria's mom had another son. Then, she met Valeria's father, an alcoholic who struggled to maintain consistent employment, with whom she had Valeria and her younger brother. During Valeria's middle school years, her father's alcoholism took a toll on the rest of his family and Valeria's life, in particular. She turned to gangs, drugs, and attempted suicide. She told me that during this time she felt lost and alone. However, her life changed when her family joined an evangelical Christian church.

Since joining the church, her father had been working relatively consistently as a day-laborer and her mother became the apartment manager of the building in which they lived. Going to church and participating in church-related activities played a major role in the life of Valeria and her family. Church services were conducted in Spanish, but the youth group was primarily conducted in English. Valeria was the only focal student who participated in an after-school activity that required her to speak Spanish. Spanish also played an important role in her life at home. Prior to entering school, she only spoke Spanish, but over the years she began to use English more frequently. Nevertheless, Valeria continued to use Spanish with

Ladson-Billings (1995) notes that successful teachers lived or spent time in the communities in which they teach. If you do not live where you teach, go shopping, eat at restaurants, or attend events in your school community. If you do live in your school community, still take some time to find events or places that you usually do not frequent. As you are spending time in the community, notice how different people are using language, think of (dis)connections between the student language use described in this chapter and what you notice. Once you return home, consider how you can add connections between the community and school in your lesson plans.

FIGURE 2.3 Create change: Noticing language use in the community

her mother. She used both languages with her friends, siblings, and father. When Valeria filled out the enrollment paperwork for her parents, she wrote that her first language and the dominant language of the adults in the house was Spanish. However, she noted that she currently uses English most frequently at home. Valeria lived a Spanish-dominant life at home and a bilingual life in other spaces.

Implications for Students Considered to be LTELs

Predominant descriptions of students considered LTELs focus on their perceived linguistic, literate, and academic deficiencies. This chapter brought a focus to students' bilingualism that challenged this type of representation. Through learning about Destiny, Eliza, Lizbeth, Jamilet, and Valeria's linguistic experiences both at home and at school, this analysis revealed that they all drew on their bilingual linguistic repertoire to engage with diverse audiences. These ways of engaging with diverse family and community members illustrated linguistic expertise that is often minimized in the literature on LTELs. In addition, this chapter reinforced existing research that shuns away from applying a singular linguistic pattern to all LTELs (Flores et al., 2015; Kibler et al., 2017). This variety among these students' linguistic experiences is particularly notable considering these five young women were selected because they were LTELs for whom English played a role in their everyday lives. Even with these criteria that were applied to the selection of the focal students, the descriptions of their linguistic histories revealed diversity in the ways both English and Spanish functioned in their lives.

While the long-term English learner label may be useful for accountability purposes, it is dangerous when it is used as a lens for teaching. It places primacy on students' official classification and the length of their classification as if it provides insight into their linguistic abilities and experiences. Moreover, it ignores the way in which raciolinguistic ideologies can function to erase students' linguistic abilities. It is more pedagogically useful to learn about students' linguistic experiences. The importance of this lesson for literacy educators is to step outside of traditional policy classifications to recognize what students bring to the classroom. However, learning about students' linguistic backgrounds if engaged in through a traditional lens where translanguaging practices are seen as deficient and the role of race is overlooked has the potential to reinforce stereotypes. As a result, this chapter provides a way of thinking about bilingualism that moves beyond the dominant lens to see so-called long-term English learners as successful users of multiple linguistic resources (Figures 2.3 and 2.4 provide concrete ways for teachers to develop this type of context-specific understanding). This understanding of their linguistic experiences is the base of the examination of the reading experiences that follows in the next three chapters.

Drawing on the previously described ideas about bilingualism and bilingual communication, the survey consists of six questions. If you want to incorporate a written component, at the end of the survey you can include a writing prompt for students to turn their responses into a descriptive paragraph about their linguistic experiences. The survey can be used with students with a wide range of bilingual experiences and in any content area. Depending on their linguistic and/or literate abilities, the survey may sometimes need to be adapted by being translated into another language or read aloud. Specifically, it could be a useful activity to engage in at the beginning of the school year.

In the following sections, I outline the six questions that constitute the survey in English and Spanish. I have used versions of this survey to inform my own instruction and as a part of research projects (e.g., Brooks, 2015). Along with each question, I include my rationale for selecting these particular areas of focus. That is, I situate my question design within examples of the research that informed my thinking.

Learning About Acquisition

Question 1: When and how did you learn your languages?

¿Cuándo y cómo aprendiste tus idiomas?

The first question, like the ones that follow, explicitly situates bilingualism as the norm by using the term *languages*. Importantly, the open-ended nature of this question allows for discussing multiple ways in which a student might have become bilingual. This framing coincides with research that has highlighted the diverse linguistic configurations of bilingual homes. For example, Romaine (1995) outlined possibilities that include families in which parents are monolingual speakers of a language that is not dominant in the broader society and families in which both parents are bilingual in a home and societal language. This survey question allows literacy educators to differentiate between students who are recent bilinguals and those who have been living with and using two languages for most of their lives.

FIGURE 2.4 Create change: A linguistically informed survey

Languages Spoken at Home

Question 2: Which languages are spoken in your home?

¿Cuáles idiomas se hablan en tu casa?

Before a student answers specific questions about who uses which languages with whom at home, this question asks the student to broadly describe his or her home linguistic environment. The question purposely avoids suggesting any particular family relationships, acknowledging that home living arrangements can include networks of related and unrelated individuals. In Valdés' (2001) study of middle school students classified as English learners (ELs), she described the living situation of one student, Lilian, who lived in a three-bedroom, one-bathroom apartment shared by 13 individuals. Lilian's nuclear family of eight, her paternal uncle's nuclear family, and two adult cousins. The answers to this survey question provide educators with an up-to-date representation of the home, which is often missing in official records.

Linguistic Interaction With Adults

Question 3: Which languages do the adults speak in your home?

¿Cuáles idiomas hablan los adultos en tu casa?

Question 4: Which languages do you use with adults in your home?

¿Cuáles idiomas utilizas con los adultos en tu casa?

This pair of questions acknowledges that in communication between adults and children, there could be multiple linguistic norms. Zentella's (1997) study of bilingualism in Puerto Rican families living in New York illustrated various ways in which adults and children interacted. Zentella noted that parents expected children to address a conversation partner in the language that the individual knew best. However, she also noted that adults and children engaged in what Gal (as cited in Zentella, 1997) referred to as *nonreciprocal conversations*. During these types of conversations, each speaker would use the language with which they felt most comfortable. Importantly, Zentella noted that differing norms were not solely based on linguistic ability. For example, language choice also represented a way to reflect identity, add emphasis, or navigate interpersonal relationships. These two survey questions reflect that a teacher's knowledge of a static linguistic identity of a household member (e.g., a Tamil speaker) does not necessarily provide insight into his or her interactions with the student.

Language Use With Young Peers

Questions 5 and 6 in the survey focus on how the student interacts with his or her peer network. Specifically, these questions are designed to understand the student's experiences with speaking.

Question 5: Which languages do you use with the young people in your home?

¿Cuáles idiomas utilizas con los jóvenes en tu casa?

Question 6: Outside of your home, which people do you speak with the most? What languages do you use with them?

¿Afuera de tu casa, con quién hablas más? ¿Qué idiomas utilizas con ellos?

FIGURE 2.4 (Cont.)

Language Use at Home With Peers

Research has suggested that the ways in which young people interact in bilingual homes can differ from the way they use language with adults. In Pease-Alvarez's (2002) study of 38 pairs of Mexican American children and parents, she found that although the focal children reported that their language use with their parents remained the same across the two interview time periods, the amount of English used with siblings increased across all groups. In other words, children reported making different linguistic choices with their siblings than with their parents. Therefore, question 5 specifically probes the ways in which the surveyed student interacts with their peer group in their home.

Language Use Outside of the Home

Question 6 was designed to gather information about language use in adolescent dominated spaces, because they can be governed by distinct linguistic norms. For example, Ibrahim (1999) described how a youth-organized picnic was a forum for adolescent girls to use English in unique ways. During the picnic, the teenage girls who were African immigrants to Canada read lyrics to U.S. R&B music and recited the lyrics together. This youth-oriented space provided an environment for students to engage in explicitly developing the linguistic features of what Ibrahim described as *Black English*, which is also known as African American English. The survey question explicitly seeks to gather information about such adolescent-centered experiences.

Contributions of the Language Survey

This survey was designed as a resource for educators learn about the linguistic experiences of their students that are absent from official school records. As a result, it is essential that this survey not be interpreted as a definitive description of students' linguistic experiences. It is a resource to develop more complex and representative descriptions of students' linguistic experiences. This more multifaceted representation can be used to inform instructional decisions that are specifically tailored to students' actual linguistic experiences. For instance, it can be used to impact to make connections with students' lives during instruction. It can also be amended to add different questions that tackle aspects of student life that you are interested in learning about.

Previously Published in "How and when did you learn your languages? Bilingual students' linguistic experiences and literacy instruction." *Journal of Adolescent & Adult Literacy*, 60(4), 383–393. Used with permission.

FIGURE 2.4 (Cont.)

3
LOCAL TEXTS
The Textual Environment of Biology and English Language Arts

> So, what I end up doing is kind of summarizing the points and main ideas through notes.
>
> *Mr. Isidro*

Alvermann (2006) asserts that all readers struggle with their comprehension of certain texts, at certain times, and in particular contexts. Drawing on the work of McDermott and Varenne (1995), she argues that the positioning of certain readers as continually "struggling" reflects a specific set of cultural assumptions about reading and society. For literacy educators, one of the most important aspects of her argument is that she highlights how the "struggling reader" label erases students' successes. Within educational research, there is a rich literature that demonstrates how *struggling reader* and other such labels render invisible the talents, abilities, and experiences of students to whom they are applied (Frankel & Brooks, 2018; Haddix, 2011; Haddix & Sealey-Ruiz, 2012; Kinloch, Burkhard, & Penn, 2017; Skerrett, 2012). The primary focus on the perceived inability of students means that the role of instructional practices and the broader schooling context that contributes to positioning students as problem readers is ignored (Gomez, 2004; Learned, 2016). Moreover, the description of young people as perpetually struggling or incapable readers facilitates dehumanizing instruction that focuses on remediation of supposed deficits, which limits students' opportunities to learn.

The notion of "struggling readers" is central to popular descriptions of the LTEL population. However, this concept does little to help educators understand what literacy education for this population should entail. In this chapter, I continue to make visible the limitations of broad and overly generic descriptions of LTELs that characterize these young people by their purported deficiencies. I do this by focusing on the texts that Destiny, Eliza, Lizbeth, Jamilet, and Valeria were asked to read in their biology and English language arts class. This emphasis on texts highlights one way in which educators can shape the instructional context to humanize reading instruction for students who are considered to be long-term English learners. Rather than focusing on individual students, this chapter examines the textual environment that characterized their everyday experiences of learning. Throughout the chapter, I highlight ways in which educators can consider what kinds of opportunities to learn currently exist in their classrooms. Finally, I close the chapter by illustrating how text sets can be used as a way to create multiple opportunities for students to engage with a range of texts that expand academic learning and include student identities.

Reading, Texts, and Comprehension

In colloquial language, the verb *to read* is considered to be *ambitransitive*. In other words, it can be used with or without a direct object. For instance, "Angelo reads." and "Angelo reads a comic book." are both grammatical statements. However, in terms of literacy pedagogy, *read* should always be a transitive verb. As an educator, it is fundamental to recognize that the nature of *what* is read affects *how* it is read (Rosenblatt, 1994). For example, the way that Angelo's history teacher expects him to read the *U.S. Bill of Rights* will differ from his geometry teacher's expectations for interpreting a word problem. This relationship between the what and how of reading is why Gee also argues that "'Read' is a transitive verb; it requires an object, a thing being read ... Learning to read is about learning to read different types of texts with real understanding" (Gee, 2004, p. 39). This idea about the significance of *what* is being read reflects a dominant perspective among literacy researchers that there is more to reading than merely being able to decode words (Ball, 2005; Frankel, Becker, Rowe, & Pearson, 2016; Gutiérrez, Morales, & Martinez, 2009; Jiménez, García, & Pearson, 1996; Neuman & Rao, 2004).

While the two examples of texts that I gave in the previous paragraph are more normative printed texts, it is necessary to acknowledge that the term *texts* is not limited to written documents. Texts can be multimodal. They can include digital, visual, and other types of resources to create and communicate meaning (Garcia, 2012; Lewis Ellison, 2017; Smith, Pacheco, & Rossato de Almeida, 2017). The texts on which this chapter focuses were those that were central to content area learning and whose primary communicative emphasis is the written/printed/digital word. I underscore *primary* communicative emphasis to describe the way that visual images, graphs, charts and other features can be significant components of texts. This emphasis allows for the recognition that multimodal documents can be fundamental to academic learning. However, I still emphasize the written/printed/digital word because of its role in determining English proficiency in the school system and its centrality to instruction in the focal classrooms.

Although I highlight the importance of the text in reading, it is necessary to recognize that it is not the only thing that is relevant for successful comprehension (e.g., Guthrie & Klauda, 2014; Greene, 2016; Ivey & Broaddus, 2001; Jiménez et al., 2015; Sciurba, 2017; Tatum, 2008). For example, Lee and Spratley (2010, p. 3) discuss the role of the text, the reader's goals, and prior knowledge. Nevertheless, this chapter focuses on the texts themselves because through an *opportunity to learn* lens students' previous experiences with different kinds of textual demands is fundamental to understanding their current reading practices (Gee, 2003; Rubinstein-Ávila, 2007; Skerrett, 2012). In addition, their future development as readers requires that they have experience with and knowledge of culturally appropriate ways of constructing meaning from various texts (Brooks & Frankel, 2018; Palincsar & Duke, 2004; Patterson, Roman, Friend, Osborne, & Donavan, 2018; Swanson et al., 2016; Wilson, Madjar, & McNaughton, 2016).

A particular way of reading being considered appropriate does not mean that it is the only nor the best way of engaging with particular text types. As the history of literacy evidences (e.g., Willis, 2007, 2015), the particular literacy practices that are considered to be appropriate are a reflection of power. Nevertheless, if students are expected to engage in particular literate practices, their classrooms should provide them with the opportunity to learn to navigate these expectations. When certain types of texts are absent from learning environments, students do not have the opportunity to learn to read them in traditional or creative and new manners. Providing students with multiple opportunities to engage with disciplinary and other meaningful texts is essential to their continual literacy development. It is for these and other reasons that adolescent literacy researchers have highlighted that students having opportunities to engage with print and nonprint texts for a variety of purposes is fundamental to research-based literacy instruction (Sturtevant et al., 2016).

Academic Texts in Mrs. Rodriguez and Mr. Gomez's Classrooms

Over the course of the academic year, I observed Destiny, Eliza, Jamilet, Lizbeth, and Valeria in two sections of Mrs. Elena Rodriguez's biology class and one section of Mr. Carlos Gomez's English language arts class. Each teacher taught courses that were identified as college-preparatory; however, they were expected to make accommodations for those students who were identified as learning English in their classrooms. Both teachers were Mexican-American Spanish-English bilinguals who were from Southern California. They shared their bilingualism and ethnic background with many of the students in these courses. In all of the periods that I observed, there were a total of 89 students. In each class, there were very few students who were not Latino—the majority of these students were Mexican American. In Mr. Gomez's English language arts class, there were two

"Black"[1] students, one of whom was also in Ms. Rodriguez's sixth period. Forty-five students were currently classified as ELs (the overwhelming majority had been in this classification since early elementary school). However, 83 were identified on official school records as coming from bilingual homes.

While students' official categorizations are useful, they did not indicate how students actually used language in their daily lives both in and out of school. Students' English language acquisition classification could not be mapped easily onto their language use in the classroom. For instance, over the course of the year, I observed students who were considered "English Only" speak Spanish on a daily basis and ELs never utter more than a couple of words in Spanish. In spite of the oral use of English and Spanish by the students, and less frequently by the teachers, the majority of the texts that students read were in English.

When I asked the focal students to describe how their schoolmates used language, they provided a description of what I witnessed every day.

Maneka: Yeah. Um … and then here at school, what languages do people speak?
Destiny: Mostly English. I don't really hear people talking Spanish.
Maneka: Yeah? So, is it that everyone speaks English all the time or how was it?
Destiny: Well, sometimes they … well, it's like something like Spanish. They are talking English and then all of a sudden they talk Spanish. And then they go back to English.
Maneka: Yeah. Is there anyone that speaks Spanish mostly?
Destiny: No.

Like Destiny, the rest of the focal students described a space in which individuals usually spoke English and sometimes integrated both languages. They acknowledged the existence of monolingual English speakers, but none could identify students who primarily spoke Spanish. Jamilet was the only student who identified one group of individuals who spoke primarily Spanish at school. She quipped, "The Spanish teachers." Bilingualism and bidialectalism were the norm at New Millennium High School.

Patterns in Overall Text Use

Both teachers engaged in oral translanguaging to different extents and in different ways. However, the texts that were used in both courses were almost exclusively in English. A notable exception was literature in Mr. Gomez's classes that sometimes included words or phrases from languages other than English. While it is often assumed that high school students will come across texts types that are associated with disciplines (e.g., Shanahan & Shanahan, 2012; Lee & Spratley, 2010), this was not the case in Destiny, Eliza, Jamilet, Lizbeth, and Valeria's biology and English language arts classes. Out of 137 biology texts[2] and 158 English language arts texts that I witnessed Mr. Gomez and Mrs. Rodriguez use during instruction,

Unique to Biology	Unique to ELA	Shared Across Both Classes
• Lab manuals	• Books	• Notes
• Textbooks	• Short stories	• Writing prompts
	• Poems	• Worksheets
	• Speeches	• Articles
		• Quizzes
		• Student-authored texts
		• Miscellaneous texts

FIGURE 3.1 Text types across biology and English language arts

only one of the top four most frequently used texts in each course was unique to the disciplinary background. In biology, these texts were lab manuals; in English language arts, the disciplinary texts were books. The three of the most common text types were shared across both classes: notes, writing prompts, and worksheets (see Figure 3.1). The most frequent text type was teacher-assembled notes. The primary differentiator between the texts used in both classes was content, not structure.

The primary written text type that was central to learning new disciplinary knowledge for the five teenagers that are the focus of this book was teacher-assembled notes. Below, I examine the construction of these predominant classroom texts. In addition, I describe the most frequent disciplinary text that students encountered: extended literary texts. The term that Mr. Gomez used to describe novels and other extended literary texts was "books." It is through the analysis of these frequently occurring texts that this chapter provides an in-depth examination of the textual environment of Destiny, Eliza, Jamilet, Lizbeth, and Valeria's biology and English language arts classrooms. These texts are important because experience with reading various text types is critical to developing specific reading practices. Therefore, knowledge of students' histories with particular text types is fundamental to understanding their current reading practices and previous opportunities to learn. Moreover, an awareness of the patterns of text usage within their own classroom is essential for educators to create opportunities to learn, build on what students know, and introduce new ideas about content.

The Predominance of Teacher-assembled Texts

Mr. Gomez and Mrs. Rodriguez were the people who created most of the texts that were used in instruction in their respective classes. I describe this process of text creation as *assembly* to account for the broad range of ways in which the two classroom teachers contributed to the construction of specific texts. Teacher-assembled texts could be divided into three categories:

1. Texts authored solely by the classroom teachers.
2. Texts authored by the classroom teachers in collaboration with colleagues.
3. Texts composed by classroom teachers integrating various segments of texts from distant authors with their own wording.

When the teacher did not assemble classroom texts, they overwhelmingly used formally published texts that were written by *distant authors*. These distant authors, such as novelists and textbook authors, do not have a direct relationship with or knowledge of the students who were reading the text. Teacher-assembled texts and texts written by distant authors represented the vast majority of written discourse with which the students were expected to make meaning. Only three times in biology and once during English language arts was there a distinct author—texts that the students themselves produced.

Teacher-assembled texts were frequently used instead of normative disciplinary texts (e.g., articles written by scientists, prose that provides historical context for novels, etc.). This text construction process meant that the Mrs. Rodriguez and Mr. Gomez relied on their existing disciplinary knowledge to create classroom texts. In addition to their disciplinary background knowledge, they also used information and text excerpts gathered from their own reading of other sources. This practice of developing texts for students was not limited to these two teachers. Other teachers whom I interviewed at New Millennium High School reported using similar strategies in their classrooms. For example, during an interview, the tenth-grade World History teacher, Mr. Isidro, shared how standardized testing affected the selection of texts that he used in his history classroom:

> I would like to do more reading, and I try to incorporate maybe two primary sources for every unit. But, with it, unfortunately, history is so standard driven I can't slow down. And, you know the readings are so much more interesting but it only covers maybe only 10% of a certain standard[3] … substandard within a whole unit standard. So, what I end up doing is kind of summarizing the points and main ideas through notes.

Mr. Isidro recognized that although reading primary sources[4] would be more engaging and, as many social studies instruction experts contend, a significant pedagogical practice (Santiago, 2019), he relied on notes that he composed because they were a more efficient method of communicating information. This practice was also not limited to New Millennium High School. Other researchers have documented this phenomenon of teachers creating texts in their work (e.g., Dillon, O'Brien, Moje, & Stewart, 2006; Greenleaf & Valencia, 2017; Hinchman, 1987; Schoenbach, Greenleaf, & Murphy, 2012; Wade & Moje, 2000).

While descriptions of frequency provide insight into various text types, it may be difficult to visualize exactly how teacher-assembled texts were constructed. To illustrate this kind of text, I include three distinct examples of teacher-assembled notes (the most common type of teacher-assembled texts students encountered). The first example is drawn from Mrs. Rodriguez's biology course and the latter two from Mr. Gomez's English language arts course. I selected two texts from Mr. Gomez's course because, unlike Mrs. Rodriguez, he employed different organizational formats. Despite different formats across classes, teacher-assembled notes on a specific instructional topic shared key similarities. They were most often used to introduce the students to new content information. Students were usually shown the pre-authored notes visually and were expected to copy them down verbatim.

Cornell Notes in Biology. Notes were an integral component of learning in Mrs. Rodriguez's classroom; they were the most frequent texts that the students used in class. Not only were they the primary method of introducing new content, but also the transcribed copies of notes in their composition books were required references for the different instructional activities in which they would later engage (Brooks, 2016).

In biology, Mrs. Rodriguez used a modified version of the Cornell Method of Note-Taking, hereafter referred to as *Cornell Notes*, to organize the text that she shared with the students. Cornell Notes traditionally comprise two columns for notes and one bottom section for a synthesis. In the traditional Cornell Note format, teachers do not author the notes; rather, students produce them as they listen to a lecture or read a text. In the notes column, students are expected to identify important information and summarize it briefly. After completing the notes, the student is expected to generate questions or keywords to write in the first column. The synthesis section is where the student writes a brief synopsis of the ideas covered in the notes.

Mrs. Rodriguez's version of Cornell Notes mirrored the traditional structure visually. For example, Valeria's copy of a slide in her composition book (see Figure 3.2) illustrates this two-column format, although she did not draw a line to divide the two columns. In Mrs. Rodriguez's class, notes were not a document that students produced independently. Mrs. Rodriguez produced the entire slide of notes that she expected students to copy. Valeria's notes reflected Mrs. Rodriguez's wording. In the right column, she copied the brief summaries written by Mrs. Rodriguez. This information was presented in sentences or phrases that were arranged via bullet points hierarchically to show their relationship to each other. She also copied Mrs. Rodriguez's pre-authored questions that appeared in the first column and provided a guiding framework with which to interpret the body of the notes. Almost all of the notes in Mrs. Rodriguez's course were presented in this format. On occasion, when the topic did not permit the information to be organized in this way, she used alternate formats, but these instances were infrequent.

Notes in English Language Arts. Notes were also an essential part of Mr. Gomez's English language arts (ELA) curriculum, but they did not play the same central role that they did in biology. Mr. Gomez used notes as a supplementary tool to present historical background information about the books the students

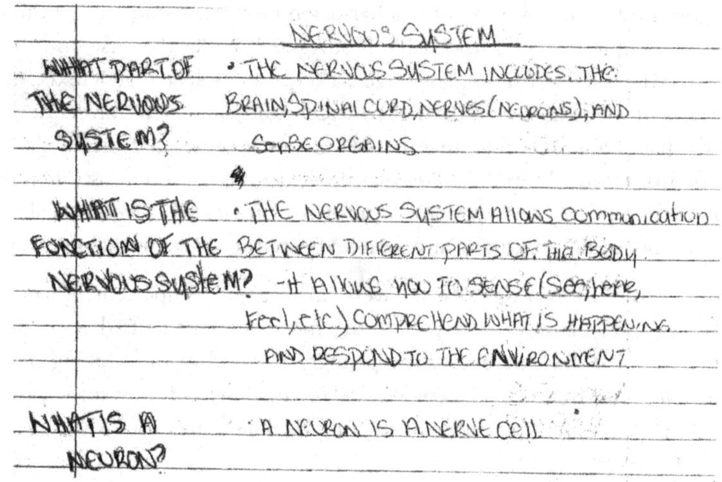

FIGURE 3.2 Valeria's notes on the nervous system

read in class as well as to teach literary devices and vocabulary words. Since they were supplementary, notes only occupied 15–20 minutes of class time on the days when they were taken. Moreover, the notes were copied on a loose sheet of paper and were designed to be used as a reference for that day's activities. That is, they were not kept in a bound composition book for the students to use as a reference later. Therefore, teacher-assembled notes were transitory texts that were relevant only for the day. However, when the notes began to address test preparation for the high school exit exam, Mr. Gomez provided folders for the students and asked them to retain and organize these written texts to prepare for the test on their own. As a result, during test preparation in the second semester, teacher-assembled notes began to occupy more class time.

Unlike Mrs. Rodriguez, Mr. Gomez did not use a specific format for notes. He changed the format of his notes according to the topic. For instance, in the excerpt of the notes that were copied by Jamilet (see Figure 3.3), he used a chart to highlight three types of conflict in literature. This chart listed brief bullet-point phrases that were separated into columns. The structure reinforced the necessary literary terms that the students would need to know to complete a text-based literary analysis project. Despite the diversity of the textual representation of notes in English language arts, there were common patterns across Mr. Gomez's various iterations of notes. Mr. Gomez, like Mrs. Rodriguez, primarily used visual devices (e.g., bullet points and titles), rather than linguistic ones, to illustrate the relationship between various phrases and brief sentences with which he wrote the body of the text. Figure 3.4 illustrates a more frequently occurring pattern of notes in ELA; the title *Jim Crow* indicates the topic. Then, each bullet point explains a specific amendment of the U.S. Constitution.

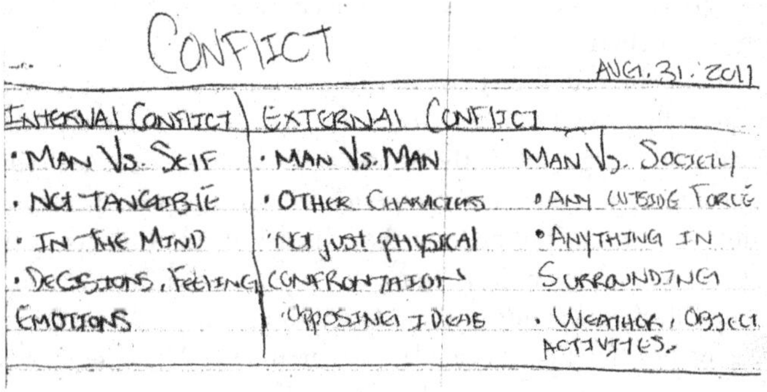

FIGURE 3.3 Jamilet's notes on literary conflict

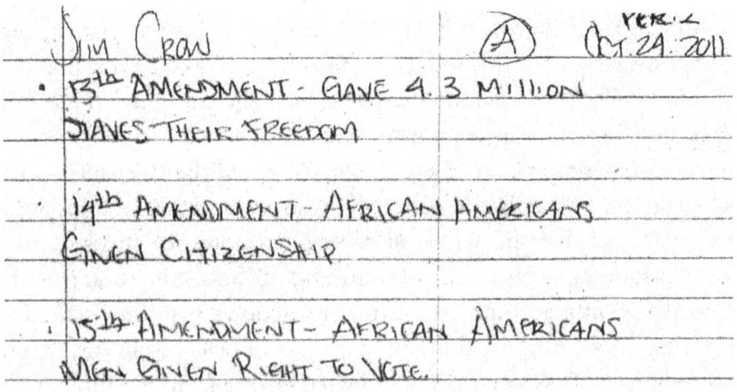

FIGURE 3.4 Jamilet's notes on Jim Crow

The previously described patterns in the selected samples of teacher-assembled notes reflect the construction of not only this text type, but also across all teacher-assembled texts that the students encountered. Although the content and form were sometimes different, teacher-assembled notes relied on similar visual devices. Moreover, they represented a significant text in both classrooms. As a result, there was a notable absence of expository texts by distant authors in the observed classes.

Teacher-Assembled Texts in the Classroom. Teacher-assembled texts were characterized by sentences or phrases relying on visual devices (e.g., bullet points and headings) for coherence. I refer to this writing style as *abbreviated*. Ninety-two percent of teacher-assembled texts were abbreviated. On the other hand, only 32% of the texts authored by distant authors employed this format. Texts by distant authors, such as books, presented students with opportunities to encounter multi-sentence and multi-paragraph discourse that adhered to dominant written conventions. While abbreviating texts is often thought of a way to make information accessible, it can actually make texts more difficult to read. For example, it can remove signals in texts that illustrate connections between ideas (Bunch et al., 2014; Pearson & Hiebert, 2014).

In addition to abbreviated text construction, teacher-assembled texts reflected Mrs. Rodriguez and Mr. Gomez's familiarity with their students. These texts reveal detailed knowledge about the students, including language background, content knowledge, and educational experiences. They appeared to be built on specific assumptions about the previous knowledge of the students in the classroom. For example, as displayed in Figure 3.3, for a unit on the nervous system, Mrs. Rodriguez illustrated an intimate understanding of her students' prior knowledge in the way she referenced vocabulary in parentheses. The content of the parentheses reflected her anticipation of the students' questions. For example, instead of using the word "neurons," Mrs. Rodriguez used a more familiar related word, "nerves." She introduced the word *neuron* to them in parentheses for the first time in these notes. Mrs. Rodriguez associated the new word, *neurons*, with a word that she felt confident that they already knew, *nerves*.[5] The second set of parentheses described the meaning of a word that she perceived they were not familiar with, "sense." The content of the parentheses described the meaning of this word by providing various examples of what it signifies.

The use of parentheses in these contexts could be viewed as happenstance. Nevertheless, through my daily observations and interactions with Mrs. Rodriguez, I learned that she wrote or redesigned notes for this specific group of tenth-grade students at New Millennium High School. She took their biology content knowledge into account, given the instructional plan they would experience in her class. Moreover, she drew on her years of teaching in this community to create a template of assumed prior knowledge that included biology content and language (e.g., vocabulary) that guided her writing of the notes. This practice was not limited to Mrs. Rodriguez. I observed both teachers rewriting notes and other texts to take the questions and misunderstandings of earlier lessons into account. Teacher-assembled texts provided an opportunity for teachers to control the texts that the students received in a very pointed way; their assembly of the texts allowed them to design texts to "invoke" the specific "addressed audience" that the students in their classroom represented (Ede & Lunsford, 1984). Both Mrs. Rodriguez and Mr. Gomez personalized teacher-assembled texts to reflect their perceptions of the language with which students were familiar, their existing content knowledge, and their previous educational experiences.

Books: A Noteworthy Disciplinary Exception

Although teacher-assembled texts were central to instruction in both classrooms, books were a significant disciplinary exception in Mr. Gomez's English language arts class. Thirty-two percent of the texts that were a part of instructional reading events in English language arts were books. During the class period, Mr. Gomez and his students usually read a section of the book that was the basis for the broader instructional unit. The books were primarily autobiographical narratives written by ethnic and/or racial minority males (e.g., Richard Wright's *Black Boy* (2007)). These books followed the male protagonist through a series of life events and integrated descriptions of these events with the author's reflections. These were tales of survival and overcoming struggles. The only book the students read that was not an autobiographical narrative was *Animal Farm* (Orwell, 2010, first published 1945). This book is an allegorical novel about the Russian Revolution of 1917, which is told through the lens of a farm with talking animals that organize a revolution against their human oppressors. Reading the assigned book usually occupied 30–35 minutes of class time, after which the students were usually asked to engage with the text in various in-class activities. This book-based reading was unique to English language arts and was central to the curriculum of Mr. Gomez's course.

The text of the books that students read generally followed the accepted patterns of narrative literary works. Several hundred pages depicted the experiences of the main character(s). These texts were organized into chapters that comprised multiple paragraphs of linguistically connected discourse. Unlike the teacher-assembled notes, the majority of the texts that the students encountered were connected multi-paragraph discourse. Books incorporated diverse literary mechanisms to accomplish their stated purpose. For example, some segments were primarily focused on description, others on dialogue, and still others contained reflective analysis. These kinds of books were the most frequent disciplinary-specific texts used in English language arts.

To illustrate how these texts were organized, I analyze selected segments from *Burro Genius: A Memoir* (Villaseñor, 2008, pp. 304–312), hereafter referred to as *Burro Genius*. In the following text excerpt, Villaseñor (2008, p. 305) relies on the visual device of beginning a new line when there was a change of speaker in the conversation. This is an accepted practice for indicating a change of speakers in literary texts.

> "But why?" I asked. My heart started beat, beat, beating. "He's the reason that our brother Joseph died," I said.
> My sister shrugged. "Yes, I know."
> "Lupe, please," our father was saying, "it's been years since *Chavaboy's* death, and life goes on. We all need to know how to let go."

While the teacher-assembled notes primarily relied on visual devices to provide an organizational structure, Villaseñor's paragraphs were not only connected through visual devices, but they were also drawn together by linguistic resources within the text. For example, when Villaseñor (2008, p. 306) is recounting his father speaking, he writes:

> Our father closed his eyes in concentration. "Lupe," he said in a very slow, gentle voice, "Jesus who is free of sin, they say, He still found it in His *corazón*

Gather lesson plans for a two-week period. These lesson plans will be used to create a chart of the texts used as a part of instructional activities. In order to identify the text types that are used in your lesson plans, start with the definition provided in this chapter (see p. 38). However, you can adjust this definition to make it work for your classroom. The goal of the chart is to be able to identify the types of texts that are used in your classroom. Once you are able to identify the texts that are most frequent, infrequent, or absent, then the next step is to consider how changing text usage can impact opportunity to learn. The chart below presents an example of such an analysis.

Text Type	Frequency
Teacher-assembled notes	✓✓✓✓✓✓✓
District-mandated textbook	✓✓✓
Scientific articles	✓✓✓✓✓
Newspaper articles	✓

FIGURE 3.5 Digging deeper: What kinds of texts do you use?

to forgive those who crucified Him. To forgive, Lupe, isn't really for the other person. It is for helping us find peace in our own hearts. I'm going up the hill to see Dr. Hoskins, and you can come with me, if you'd like."

In this passage, he employs punctuation and linguistic devices to connect the text internally. The quotation marks signal that these are not the narrator's words. The writing outside of the quotation marks indicates who is speaking. The first sentence of the passage directs the reader's attention to the father as a focal character. Later, Villaseñor describes how the words in the quotation marks were spoken and refers to the speaker as "he." Using the lens provided by Halliday and Hasan (1976), this is an example of pronominal reference cohesion. From the broader textual organization of chapters, to visual devices like indentation, to the more fine-tuned use of punctuation and linguistic connections, these ways of creating links among texts reflect predominant academic conventions. The previously described ways of organizing text were not unique to Villaseñor, however, they were also characteristic of the other books that the students encountered in English language arts.

Implications for Students Considered to be LTELs

Mrs. Rodriguez and Mr. Gomez cared deeply about their students' success. Mrs. Rodriguez wanted them to know biology content so that they could love science as much as she did. Mr. Gomez was committed to students in his community and wanted to see them excel. The carefully constructed texts that they made on a daily basis illustrated the depth of their commitment. However, it is necessary to consider what this predominant practice meant for students' opportunity to learn.

The predominance of teacher-assembled texts in Destiny, Eliza, Lizbeth, Jamilet, and Valeria's biology and English language arts classrooms created dominant patterns of text composition that was distinct from both disciplinary traditions and general academic writing (Fang, 2008; Fang & Schleppegrell, 2010; Patterson et al., 2018; Scarcella, 2003). The predominant texts in the focal students' biology and English language arts classrooms were guided by a distinct academic norm that relied heavily on teacher-assembled texts and were characterized by the following attributes:

1. Academic texts were composed of individual sentences/phrases that rely on visual devices to indicate the relationships between ideas.
2. Academic texts explicitly and directly connected with the reader's background knowledge.

Moreover, the demands of these texts were drastically different from the extended texts written by distant authors that they undoubtedly encountered on standardized English literacy exams, which were used as assessments of academic achievement and English language proficiency, and that influenced their academic trajectory.

In their biology and English language arts classes, Destiny, Eliza, Jamilet, Lizbeth, and Valeria had few opportunities to read texts that follow more normative disciplinary traditions. Mr. Gomez's use of books was the only recurring use of a text produced by a distant author that was a consistent part of classroom life. Although they relied on more traditional organizational structures, the texts were primarily autobiographical narratives. While autobiographical narratives are an essential element of an English language arts classroom, multiple experiences with many different kinds of texts were absent from both classrooms.

The focal students' minimal interaction with texts written by distant authors and their diverse text structures, and thus their similarly restricted opportunities to learn ways in which these texts are read, could hinder their meaning-making practices. For example, Goldman and Rakestraw (2000) assert that when encountering unfamiliar content, readers can rely on their knowledge of text structure to help them interpret this unknown information. In the case of the focal students, their experiences with teacher-assembled texts suggests that they might be less likely to rely on text structure as a meaning-making resource when they encountered unfamiliar material in texts that reflected the more dominant academic conventions. Their ability to rely on prior knowledge of text structure would be restricted to the narrative texts that characterize the literature they encountered in English language arts classes. This unfamiliarity with diverse text types would be even more pronounced if their experiences with teacher-assembled texts were mirrored in other classes, like World History, to which Mr. Isidro alluded at the beginning of this chapter.

Next Steps

This chapter highlights the importance of students' opportunities to learn from different text types. One way to change the textual environment is through the use of text sets. A teacher creates a text set when they bring together multiple curricular resources to support learning. However, using text sets requires more than just grabbing different texts and giving them to students at the same time. Texts sets can have a variety of purposes that shape which texts are used, how learning is measured, and the activities in which students engage with them (Hartman & Hartman, 1994). They are not just a way to provide students with access to multiple texts for the sake of exposure. They are deeply intertwined with learning. Therefore, it is important to know how the text set will be used within the curriculum. I close this chapter by providing educators with two types of text sets that can be used to build background knowledge: quad text set (Lupo, Strong, Lewis, Walpole, & McKenna, 2018) and linked text set (Elish-Piper, Wold, & Schwingendorf, 2014). Prior to discussing how text sets can be used for particular goals and building off of Mr. Gomez and Mrs. Rodriguez's teaching practices in this chapter, I argue that it is imperative for educators to understand what text types they are already using in their classrooms and what are possible texts they can include in text sets.

Earlier in this chapter, Figure 3.5 asked readers to analyze the nature of text usage to see patterns. These patterns in text usage help identify frequently relied upon texts. This allows educators to consider what "academic texts" look like in their classroom and to consider how the textual environment reflects curricular and other goals for students. In addition to thinking about what text types students are reading, it is necessary to think about who is writing the texts that students are being asked to read and what views are being represented in the text set (Souto-Manning, 2017). Figure 3.6 includes some questions that educators can ask themselves about the diversity of perspectives that exists in the current textual base that students are asked to read. These questions are also significant to ask of the texts that will be included in future text sets. Humanizing reading instruction requires that multiple perspectives are a regular part of everyday classroom teaching and learning.

In addition to considering what texts are currently being used in a classroom, it is necessary to be aware of the number of possibilities of texts that can be used. State curriculum standards, professional organizations, and practitioner-focused research are places to look for text types that should be included in text set design moving forward. In addition, the texts that students choose to engage with in their out-of-school lives can be included within a text set. Figures 3.6 and 3.7 include guidance for the identification of possible text types to use as a part of constructing new text sets. The guidance ensures that the texts to which students have access are not only dictated by standards and testing, but also students' daily lives and community needs. This explicitly brings reading instruction back to

Consider the texts that you like to use most frequently. What are the gender, racial/ ethnic, and linguistic identities of these authors?

- Look up information about the authors to make sure that you are not only using resources that are written by a single type of author.
- Explicitly look for resources that bring the perspectives of different backgrounds into your classroom.
  - ◦ What perspectives are privileged within the text set?
  - ◦ What perspectives are absent from the text set?
- Look online for professional resources that may have already identified these types of texts.

FIGURE 3.6 Digging deeper: Textual analysis

- Review your state content standards or the standards for a reputable professional organization. What types of texts do these standards indicate that you should use?
  - ◦ Can you find these text types in your lesson plan?
  - ◦ What other text types can you incorporate into your instructional repertoire?
  - ◦ What resources will you need to access these types of texts?
- Learn about the texts that your students enjoy out-of-school and within school.
  - ◦ What do they find engaging about these texts?
  - ◦ What patterns do you notice about their responses?
  - ◦ Can you incorporate similar text types or features from these texts into your classroom?
  - ◦ Remember that students can engage with texts in many languages. Do not limit yourself to English!

FIGURE 3.7 Create change: What kinds of texts can you use?

creating relationships between student, teacher, and school, which is central to humanizing work (Edwards et al., 2016).

Once an educator understands the patterns of text usage and what text types can be incorporated into a text set, then next focus should be on why and how a text set is being used. In the next section, I describe two ways to build text sets to develop and refine background knowledge. These are not the only ways text sets can be used. However, they are two ways that are useful across content areas.

Text Sets to Build Background Knowledge

Lupo et al. (2018) describe an insightful way of using text sets to encourage students to read challenging texts through building background knowledge. Their way of organizing texts sets is called the "Quad Text Set Framework." This way of organizing text sets involves selecting a single text that is challenging for students to read. The remaining three text sets are designed to develop background knowledge and motivation to read the *challenging* text. Specifically, they suggest that the three remaining texts come from one of each of the following text types: visual or video, informational, accessible (these texts are related to youth and popular culture). Moreover, they note that providing students with opportunities to reread the *challenging* text after engaging with other texts allowed for greater depth of understanding.

As an example, they illustrate a text set that incorporates all of these characteristics within a history lesson about the First Amendment to the U.S. Constitution (Lupo et al., 2018, p. 441): visual text: "The Bill of Rights: The first Amendment" by Keith Hughes (YouTube); informational text: "Citizenship and the Internet" in *Civics Today* (textbook chapter); accessible text: "Donald Trump Threatens to Sue the Times Over Article on Unwanted Advances" by Alan Rappeport in the New York Times; and target text: case study based on the *Tinker v. Des Moines School District* (1969) case on high school students wearing armbands to protest the Vietnam War. In this way, students are adding to the existing knowledge that they have so that they can tackle texts that may have previously been perceived as too challenging.

Linked Text Sets

The concept of linked text sets (Elish-Piper et al., 2014) is akin to the previously described way of creating text sets to develop background knowledge. However, within this model there is a more explicit focus on beginning with what is typically referred to as students' out-of-school literacies (e.g., popular music, YouTube videos, and short stories) as a way to access and build background knowledge for challenging texts. The authors note:

> Linked text sets provide a three-pronged process for developing student interest and providing appropriate scaffolding to read a variety of texts at the high school level. With this approach, we first *engage* students in texts that link to their lived experiences and provide scaffolding toward more complex texts ... Then we encourage students to *explore* texts for connections to their lives and to think critically about the significance of the ideas presented in the texts. Finally, we provide opportunities for students to *expand* on what they know and are learning by synthesizing themes across multiple texts.
>
> *Elish-Piper et al., 2014, p. 567, emphasis added*

They refer to the key stages in this type of text set as engagement, exploration, and expansion. Moreover, this type of text set is united by an essential question (McTighe, Seif, & Wiggins, 2004) that reflects students' lives and the goals of instruction. The example they provide that relates to English language arts is a linked text set that addresses the question: Why is growing up so difficult? Through considering these phases, teachers are explicitly tackling student engagement and opportunity to learn.

Closing

Text sets are a hands-on approach through which students can interact with a variety of texts. Moreover, they allow teachers to build in multiple voices and various entry points into a subject matter. This helps to ensure that students' lives and interests are a part of the curriculum. Lastly, they ensure rigorous interaction with a range of texts. This kind of instruction is central to students considered to be LTELs' opportunity to learn.

Notes

1 One student was African American; the other was the child of Belizean immigrants.
2 Although I observed two periods of biology, I counted each text only once. This includes all classroom observations in which at least one focal student was present.
3 He is referencing the California Standards for History/Social Studies.
4 Primary sources are artifacts, or reproductions of artifacts, that were produced during a particular historic period of study. These are not limited to written texts, but can include documents, such as the *Declaration of Independence*.
5 *Nerves* and *neurons* are not synonyms. However, they are related to each other.

4

STRONG AND LOUD READERS

Academic Reading in the Classroom[1]

No, like her reading and then her picking a person she reads, like popcorn.

Destiny Lopez

While the last chapter provided insight into what texts were a part of Destiny, Eliza, Jamilet, Lizbeth, and Valeria's learning environment, it did not describe the reading practices that students used to make meaning from these texts. Drawing on the literacy as social practice perspective, this chapter examines these reading practices. Reading practices include what individuals do with reading and the beliefs that they hold about reading—both observable and unobservable (Street, 2012). However, this chapter primarily focuses on the *observable* reading practices that occurred during instruction and what they reveal about the nature of academic reading in these classrooms. These meaning-making practices are part of what Bloome (2008, p. 251) refers to as the *official literacy practices* of each classroom. These practices are significant because the social interaction between teacher, students, and text are fundamental to understanding what the focal students are learning about reading in academic contexts (Street, 2008). In the local context, these practices constituted *academic reading*.

The three rules guiding academic reading in Mrs. Rodriguez and Mr. Gomez's classrooms were: (1) reading involves more than one person; (2) reading entails making meaning aloud; and (3) reading means that the teacher will provide an official interpretation. In spite of students' official classification as English learners, these instructional practices created an environment in which educators demonstrated confidence in students' oral English language abilities by relying on them to comprehend written texts. As a result, the focal students' everyday schooling experiences did not provide students with the opportunity to practice reading texts independently, whether they be teacher-assembled or written by distant authors.

While the previously described reading practices were successful in sharing content area knowledge; they did not prepare students to silently and independently comprehending texts. The ability to silently and independently comprehend texts is a vital reading practice for adolescents and adults. For adolescent students who are considered to be learning English, it is a primary reading practice through which their English language proficiency is assessed (e.g., TELPAS, ELPA21, and WIDA). It is fundamental to assessments that are required for entry to many colleges and universities, like the ACT and SAT. Moreover, silent reading is a more efficient way to comprehend texts because one is not limited by the rate at which they can produce speech (Hiebert, Wilson, & Trainin, 2010). As a result, silent reading is a way to rapidly process texts that students can encounter both in and outside of school.

Similar to the overreliance on specific text types in the previous chapter, the predominance of oral reading in groups in which the teacher provides an official interpretation of the meaning created an absence of opportunity to learn. Specifically, it provided minimal opportunities for students to engage in individual and silent meaning-making with texts. Moreover, the focus on the teacher providing the official interpretation leaves little room for student agency. It positions students as recipients, rather than co-constructors, of knowledge. In this chapter, I continue to move the emphasis from a generic focus on students as struggling readers to the predominant reading practices that characterized their schooling experiences. This emphasis calls attention to what educators are teaching students about how to read and what they can do to ensure the reading practices of the classroom prepare students to critically engage with texts that they will encounter. Throughout the chapter, I highlight how educators can evaluate the kinds of opportunities to silently and independently comprehend texts that exist in their current or will exist in their future classrooms. Finally, I close the chapter by illustrating how educators can support students' individual engagement with texts. Specifically, these strategies rely on recognizing student voice and previous experiences which is central to humanizing education (Irizarry, 2017).

Academic Reading in Practice

The primary reading practices on which the focal teachers relied to engage students with texts involved oral meaning-making in groups that included reading aloud and the teacher providing an oral interpretation of the test. It is necessary to acknowledge that these reading practices were not unique to the classrooms I observed or New Millennium High School. Wade and Moje's (2000) review of reading research identifies the importance of teachers' "oral texts" in subject-area classrooms. In an earlier review, Alvermann and Moore (1991, p. 969) highlighted how research suggests that teachers' "governance of students' encounters with print" characterizes much of secondary school pedagogy. In addition, research published since Wade and Moje highlight the ongoing presence of this practice (Albright & Ariail, 2005; Alvermann, 2018; Ariail & Albright, 2006; Brooks & Frankel, 2018; Klecker & Pollock, 2005; Swanson et al., 2016; Valdés, Lomelí, Taube & Teachers of Latino College Preparatory Academy, 2017). Moreover, the focal students and their teachers reported similar reading practices in other instructional spaces. For example, Destiny provided the following description of the typical classroom practices for academic reading in her eighth-, ninth-, and tenth-grade English language arts courses:

Maneka: So how would you compare English this year to English last year?

Destiny: I think English last year was way easier. 'Cuz you would take notes, but a little bit. It was like mostly reading or paying attention.

Maneka: Yeah and then how about compared to eighth grade?

Destiny: It was easier. 'Cuz well with my eighth-grade teacher, you wouldn't really do much but read and that's about it.

Maneka: And when you say read, how would you guys read?

Destiny: Like the book or *Romeo and Juliet*.

Maneka: But, would you read it like in class individually or would you read it out loud…

Destiny: Out loud.

Maneka: Everybody together…

Destiny: Usually the teacher…

Maneka: Oh, the teacher…

Destiny: Yeah, the teacher.

Maneka: The teacher would read it out loud. And then what would you guys do?

Destiny: We would just like listen or take notes. And then she'll stop and explain us.

Maneka: And then in ninth grade, how would you guys read?

Destiny: In the class, like everyone together.

Maneka: Everyone together at the same time?

Destiny: No, like her reading and then her picking a person she reads, like popcorn.

Maneka: And then, how would you describe how you read now in Mr. Gomez?

Destiny: Well … it's nothing different. It is the same thing. Popcorn reading.

During this interview segment, Destiny characterized academic reading as reflecting the three rules of classroom reading that I had observed in her tenth-grade biology and English language arts courses. Not only did Destiny's description reflect the previously described *three rules of academic reading*. It was also similar

It is important to consider how your own experiences with literacy in high school may shape the way you teach or think about using texts. Take a moment to reflect on your own high school learning experiences. Then, consider the following questions:

• What did reading look like in your subject area?

• How did these experiences prepare or not prepare you for college?

• How do your experiences compare to the students in this book?

• What impact do you think these types of reading experiences could have on the focal students' educational trajectories?

After you have considered these questions, share your thoughts with someone else who has also read this book. Discussing your experiences with and ideas about literacy instruction provides a context to reflect on the interconnections between your personal educational journey and pedagogical practices.

FIGURE 4.1 Digging deeper: Your high school literacy experiences

to the descriptions of Eliza, Jamilet, Lizbeth, Valeria, and the other teachers that I interviewed. The major distinction between the focal students' and teachers' representation of reading is that the teachers did not expressly describe providing oral summaries of texts. (See Figure 4.1 for the opportunity to explore your own reading history.)

In order to move from these broad patterns to specific examples of academic reading in biology and English language arts, I situate the previous descriptions within two vignettes. The first vignette is based on the abbreviated teacher-assembled notes in biology that were discussed in Chapter 3. The second involves another frequent text type: a section of a novel from English language arts. However, this represents a distinct section of text than that which was analyzed in the previous chapter. These descriptive vignettes are designed to identify the nature of the meaning-making practices that were required of students and teachers. Therefore, at the end of each vignette, I will make the role of teacher and student in meaning-making explicit.

An Introduction to the Nervous System

In the following excerpt, I describe how the teacher-assembled notes from biology were read during class.[2] Although these notes comprised several slides in the PowerPoint deck, the following description focuses only on the first slide. These notes depict the first time that Mrs. Rodriguez planned to explicitly teach the students about the nervous system. Previously, they had learned concepts about the nervous system as part of a more general activity about the various organ systems of the human body. This lesson was different from that introductory overview because the students were presented with the detailed information that was required for the state standardized test and asked to complete a lab about reflexes at the end of the period. Although Eliza is the only focal student who participated verbally in the discussion, both Destiny and Lizbeth were present during this class period.

After spending several minutes attempting to get the attention of the students, who were still chatting about the previous instructional activity, Mrs. Rodriguez loaded the PowerPoint presentation onto the screen in front of the classroom. Only the title of the initial slide—"Nervous System"—was visible to the students; this moment was when written text was first involved in this instructional activity (see Figure 3.2). Mrs. Rodriguez began meaning-making with the text by reading the title aloud.

> **Mrs. Rodriguez**: All right, so the nervous system. So, today we are going to finish … um we are going to talk about the nervous system. We are going to take about ten minutes of notes, and then you guys are going to do a lab. You are going to do a quick lab to test your reflexes. How fast are your reflexes? All right … so let me get my Popsicle sticks.
> [In order to ensure that she called on students equally, Mrs. Rodriguez had Popsicle sticks with each student's name on them. She would select sticks from a cup to identify which student would be called on to answer her questions.]
> **Mrs. Rodriguez**: Eliza, what do you think is a part of your nervous system?
> [Another student begins to answer Mrs. Rodriguez's question.]
> **Mrs. Rodriguez**: Eliza. Eliza.
> **Eliza**: Your nerve cells.
> **Mrs. Rodriguez**: Your nerve cells. What else? What other kinds of things work with your nerve cells?
> **Other students**: Your brain! Your muscles?
> **Mrs. Rodriguez**: And then, what else is one thing that is aligning or connecting all your nerve cells?
> **Several students in unison:** Your spine.

Once Mrs. Rodriguez heard the answer she was looking for, she repeated the title of the notes and pulled up the first bullet point, which read, "The nervous system includes the brain, spinal cord, nerves (neurons), and sense organs." Then, the students began to copy this line of text as Mrs. Rodriguez read part of the bullet point, which she followed with oral explanations of information that was not present on the slide.

> **Mrs. Rodriguez:** This includes your brain, your spinal cord, your nerves, which are also called neurons, and it also includes your sense organs. So, like so the things in your body that allow you to sense something. So, your skin like when you touch something hot, your skin sensed it. When you eat too much sugar, your liver senses it and does something with your nervous system. When you work out, your muscles are working, and you feel that pain. All organs that sense something are also a part of your nervous system.

So, you got a brain that is the main one. You have your spinal cord and you have all of your nerves all of those connections with your body. So, now with that, Hugo, what do you think the nervous system does?

At the end of the previous transcript, Mrs. Rodriguez asked Hugo what appeared to be an open-ended question. However, this question began an interaction in which she attempted to guide him into stating the information that she wrote on the still unseen second bullet point.

Hugo: Controls your nerves.
Mrs. Rodriguez: Controls your nerves. So, what do your nerves do? What do you think the function of the nervous system is?
Hugo: Keep you stable.
Mrs. Rodriguez: Yeah, everything is going to keep you stable. Yeah, but like what would be the role of the brain, your nerves, and your spinal cord? What are all three of those trying to do?
Cristina: [Inaudible]
Mrs. Rodriguez: What do you think your brain tries to do?
Ivan: React.
Guillermo: It tries to send a message.
Mrs. Rodriguez: So, we got it, tries to send a message, react. [Adrián is raising his hand. She looks to him.] What was yours?
Adrián: That your brain and your nervous system connects neurons to like your nerves and so then you like react or whatever.
Mrs. Rodriguez: Yes, so they are going to send messages. They are going to react. So, what they do is they allow communication between different parts of our body. Your nervous system is responsible for communicating…

When Adrián brought up an idea that was connected to what she had prepared in the notes, Mrs. Rodriguez revealed the next bullet point to the students. This bullet point read, "The nervous system allows communication between different parts of the body." She recited most of the text on the slide and added details and explanations that were not written down. She continued with this pattern for the next sub-bullet point and final sentence on the slide that read, "It allows you to sense (see, hear, feel, etc.), comprehend what is happening, and respond to the environment." At the end of this section of the PowerPoint slides, Mrs. Rodriguez had orally interpreted all of the bullet points for the students. That is, in addition to reading what was on the slide, she expanded on this information in her oral discourse.

In order to incorporate the question-creating aspect of Cornell Notes, Mrs. Rodriguez called on individual students to design questions that provided organization and context for the bullet points. Although the students were asked to create the questions, Mrs. Rodriguez inputted questions that she wrote on the slide. She made her version of the question on the PowerPoint slide visible after a student shared a related, self-created question.

> **Mrs. Rodriguez**: So, Horacio over here. What do you think the first question is?
>
> **Horacio**: What does um … the nervous system um … what does the nervous system include?
>
> **Mrs. Rodriguez**: Yeah, what does the nervous system include? [She brought up the question on the PowerPoint.] What does the nervous system include? What is part of the nervous system? Good job. So, what is part of the nervous system or what does it include … Carolina, what about the second bullet point?
>
> **Carolina**: What does the nervous system allow?
>
> **Mrs. Rodriguez**: Okay. What does the nervous system allow? What is the job of the nervous system? [She brought up the second question on the PowerPoint.] What is the function of the nervous system? So, what does it allow us to do? How does it allow us to react?

The two pre-entered questions that Mrs. Rodriguez had written were, "What is part of the nervous system?" and "What is the function of the nervous system?" She rephrased the students' responses into the pre-existing questions that were now visible in the text. Once Mrs. Rodriguez pulled up the second question, the slide had been completely read. This process was repeated for the remainder of the slides in the PowerPoint deck. Once all of the slides had been completed, the students were asked to write a synthesis statement in response to a prompt.

What "Counts" as Reading? Notes in Biology and English Language Arts. In this snapshot of meaning-making in action, the students were visually presented with a written text. This text was read aloud to them. It was not read verbatim, but it was integrated into a larger segment of oral discourse that included additional details and paraphrasing. Mrs. Rodriguez interpreted the text in conjunction with her background knowledge using an oral explanation. Table 4.1 illustrates how the students saw one text, but also heard distinct oral discourse. As a result, comprehending written text involved the participation of a more knowledgeable guide. The role of the student in this meaning-making process is to attend to the oral interpretation, while copying down the text that s/he sees visually. The few exceptions in which the student participated in making meaning occurred when s/he was called upon to develop a question or if s/he volunteered to participate. However, the teacher still had the final say in the determining meaning. This pattern of reading teacher-assembled notes was the most common reading practice in Mrs. Rodriguez's biology class (Brooks, 2016).

Reading teacher-assembled notes shared many meaning-making practices across biology and English language arts. Mr. Gomez orally interpreted the text

TABLE 4.1 Students see/students hear: Biology notes

Students See	Students Hear
The nervous system includes the brain, spinal cord, nerves (neurons), and sense organs.	This includes your brain, your spinal cord, your nerves, which are also called neurons, and it also includes your sense organs. So, like so the things in your body that allow you to sense something. So, your skin, like when you touch something hot your skin sensed it. When you eat too much sugar your liver senses it and does something with your nervous system. When you work out your muscles are working and you feel that pain. All organs that sense something are also a part of your nervous system. So, you got a brain that is the main one. You have your spinal cord and you have all of your nerves all of those connections with your body. So, now with that Hugo. What do you think the nervous system does?

for the students. The role of students in this instructional reading event involved listening to oral interpretations of a written text and guidance from a more knowledgeable instructor. They were provided with more information orally than was found in the teacher-assembled notes. While listening to the teacher interpret the text orally, they were expected to copy what they saw.

While there were many ways in which reading teacher-assembled notes were similar, there were two minor differences that must be mentioned. Mr. Gomez did not use Cornell Notes; therefore, the students' reading notes did not include the question development or synthesis statement components. The second difference is that Mr. Gomez sometimes asked the students to recite the notes aloud and provided his interpretation following their oral recitation. As a result, sometimes the students' role in classroom reading included reading aloud. However, these differences did not alter the fact that the teachers' oral discourse was the "text" from which students were expected to receive the official meaning while "doing notes."

"Effective" Reading in English Language Arts

These previously illustrated reading practices represent the patterns associated with using abbreviated teacher-assembled texts in the classroom. Therefore, it is possible that the reliance on oral language for text comprehension was characteristic for only these text types. They included sentences and phrases that were usually organized using visual devices (e.g., bullet points). This pattern could mean that the nature of this text construction required an oral interpretation by the assembler (the teacher). Therefore, in the next section, I examine the dominant reading practices involved in making meaning with extended multi-paragraph texts written by distant authors. Specifically, I share a vignette that illustrates how the most frequent extended multi-paragraph text—"a book"—with which the focal students interacted was read.

After attempting to gain the attention of his talkative class several times, Mr. Gomez finally began to review the agenda for the day. First on the to-do list was to complete an introductory activity that required students to reflect, in writing, on *Burro Genius* (Villaseñor, 2008), then they were to finish reading Villaseñor's book, and class ended with Mr. Gomez introducing the final essay for the unit. This analysis highlights the section of class during which they read *Burro Genius*.

The students knew what to do when Mr. Gomez said, "page 305." Most of the class got out their edition of *Burro Genius*. Once most of the students had their books out and opened to page 305, Mr. Gomez began with the customary oral summary of the previous night's reading. The overwhelming majority of reading took place in class, but Mr. Gomez also assigned two to three pages of reading as homework. The ritual of in-class summaries suggested that he was aware that most students did not actually read the assigned pages.

Rather than providing the students with a summary, Mr. Gomez invited students to join him in summarizing the reading, which he led through posing strategic questions. Jamilet, uncharacteristically, had brought her book to class and completed the previous night's homework. Her father had met with the Spanish teacher, Ms. Alvarado, about her disruptive behavior during class. Subsequently, for a couple of days, she had remained intently engaged in most of her courses. Therefore, she participated more frequently than usual in the following interaction.

> **Mr. Gomez**: For your homework reading, I did a quick plot triangle. [He pointed to the whiteboard on which he had drawn a plot triangle with key events.] It starts off where he stands up to that kid in the bus. He finally goes crazy on him. He's like, "Let's fight! Let's fight!" The bus driver says, "Ay, I am going to do a report." Victor says, "Report it! I'll report you too! What's the bus driver say? "Oh forget about it!"
> [Several students laugh.]
> **Mr. Gomez**: There is no report, okay. He then finds a hobby.
> **Selena**: Wrestling.
> **Mr. Gomez**: Wrestling, right? He starts lifting weights. He gets into wrestling. He finds out that he is really good at it, and he starts feeling good about himself.
> **Isabel**: Don't forget about Moses.
> **Mr. Gomez**: But, then he goes to class.

Isabel: There he is.

Jamilet: Then he sees the playboy girl.

Mr. Gomez: And Moses pretty much humiliates Victor. Um, he has a magazine of a girl and he is like tryna trying to like embarrass him, which works. Victor doesn't really want to say nothing because he respects women.

Jamilet: And they think that he is gay.

Mr. Gomez: Well, they started insulting him.

Isabel: They thought he was…

Mr. Gomez: Right? They start insulting him in his own classroom. His own teacher is leading it. So, Victor runs home and wants to get…

Ofelia: A weapon.

Mr. Gomez: A weapon. He is gonna run and get a weapon and his plan is to come back to the school. Okay?

After Mr. Gomez led several students in building an oral summary of the events that happened immediately prior to the text that would be read in class, he drew their attention to the book by saying, "So, we are going to start off at the bottom of 304. Okay, Mr. Adán go ahead and start us of bottom of 304, where it says, 'I was not sixteen years old.'" This was when the written text became a part of the meaning-making practice. Adán began to read, then Mr. Gomez read, then he called on a different student to read. This practice was a modified version of what is traditionally called *round-robin reading*. In round-robin reading, the teacher selects different students to read aloud. However, I qualify this practice by calling it "modified" because Mr. Gomez was not only the selector of the student who reads, but he also did most of the reading himself. After several instances of turn-taking, in which Mr. Gomez read longer stretches of text than the student readers, he paused and asked the students to help him summarize. Isabel and Ofelia delivered the summary.

After the summary, Mr. Gomez asked them to complete their reading notes. Reading notes involved students providing written evidence that they had used the Seven Habits of Effective Readers. These habits included: asking questions, making meaning, visualizing, activating schema, determining importance, synthesizing, and drawing inferences. Mr. Gomez learned about these seven habits at a professional development seminar and diligently incorporated them into his instructional repertoire.

Typically, Mr. Gomez reintroduced the reading notes to the students by writing the options on the board and orally reminding them what each note might contain.

Mr. Gomez: Go ahead and title it "notes." Notes, *Burro Genius* … We got "making meaning" is something you don't understand, questions, "visualize" is drawing, synthesizing—tell me what is going on, "determining importance" is a quote, "activating schema" is the connections, and "drawing inference" is a prediction. Just do one note, please, of your choice.

	Burro Genius
ASKing Question	why didn't victor's dad get mad when he told him that he was going to flunk again?
Visualize	
Synthesise	Victor's dad is really Drunk but not only him his here is drunk to su then victor and his mom so get his dad to the cantina but he does not want to come home.
ASKing Question	who is the lady that is going to hold the horse?

FIGURE 4.2 Lizbeth's "effective" reading notes

There was no explicit expectation about the length of the students' responses or how the comments should be phrased. Figure 4.2 illustrates an example of notes on a different section[3] of *Burro Genius*. However, he did attempt to dissuade the students from relying on the option of visualizing that entailed the students making a drawing. The focal students' written responses included brief phrases, words, and sentences. They rarely extended beyond one sentence.

Once the reading note was completed, Mr. Gomez selected another student to read, and the modified round-robin reading continued until they reached another point for summarizing and reading notes. That time, Mr. Gomez provided the summary and did not ask for student participation. This process of modified round-robin reading, interspersed with summaries, continued until the assigned reading was finished. At the end of this activity, all of the reading had been completed aloud; Mr. Gomez was the most frequent reader as well as the *official* interpreter of meaning.

What "Counts" as Reading? Reading Books in English Language Arts.
The previous vignette began with Mr. Gomez summarizing the previous night's reading assignment. This practice of summarizing relied primarily on his oral summaries, the plot triangle he constructed, and his strategic questioning of student volunteers. Once again, Mr. Gomez did most of the meaning-making and students were expected to listen to his interpretation and participate only if called upon to

do so. Later instances of summarizing did not use the same resources as this initial interaction; they relied more heavily on Mr. Gomez's strategic questioning of students who volunteered. Superficially, it may appear that these kinds of summaries were distinct from the teacher-driven summaries provided with teacher-assembled notes because students who responded to Mr. Gomez's questions participated in constructing meaning from the text that they had heard (and read). Nevertheless, it was similar to Mrs. Rodriguez's creation of Cornell Notes questions because by posing specific questions and waiting to hear an interpretation with which he agreed, Mr. Gomez was still providing the official interpretation of the text. When the actual role of the text became more evident in the vignette, the way in which reading took place differed from what transpired based on the teacher-assembled notes. Mr. Gomez treated the book as a script to be read verbatim.

While Mrs. Rodriguez and Mr. Gomez integrated additional details that were not present in the written text as they read their notes aloud, this activity did not occur while reading books in the English language arts class. Mr. Gomez's read-alouds of books treated the text as a script for oral recitation. Occasionally, he would change words or add extraneous details for humor. Sometimes, he would pause to clarify a particular term or sentence that he felt might be confusing for the students. Mr. Gomez demonstrated such an aside when he began reading the text where Adán left off. "Six huge bucks, which are like deers, six huge bucks, I'd gotten this last year, and right now I was going to use a little .22 to do in Moses." In this section of the read-aloud, Mr. Gomez quickly realized that the one of the first couple sentences used an unfamiliar term: *bucks*. Therefore, in the midst of reciting the text orally, he provided an aside with a clarification of the word using a more common and related term: *deer*. It was unusual for Mr. Gomez to insert his own words directly into the text he was reading aloud; Table 4.2 illustrates that there was greater congruence between what the students saw in the text of the book and what they heard being read aloud. When it was the students' turn to read, however, they did not incorporate the clarifying asides. They read the text word-for-word as it was written. Their adaptations of the text usually occurred when they skipped over a word that they did not know or misread a word that was spelled similarly.

Although books were treated as scripts, they were not free of the teacher's official interpretation of meaning. As described earlier, Mr. Gomez's summaries still

TABLE 4.2 Students see/students hear: *Burro Genius*

Students See	Students Hear
Six huge bucks, I'd gotten this last year. I was a crack-shot with a rifle or pistol, and right now I was going to use a little .22 to do in Moses.	Six huge bucks, *which are like deers,* six huge bucks, I'd gotten this last year. I was a crack-shot with a rifle or pistol, and right now I was going to use a little .22 to do in Moses.

provided an official evaluation of the text. Students had three options about how to make meaning with the text:

1. They could listen to the oral recitation and interpretation.
2. They could look at the text and listen to the oral recitation and interpretation.
3. They could engage in one of the two previously described options and recite the text aloud when called upon (this option was only available to selected students).

For this reason, the positioning of effective reading notes after Mr. Gomez had interpreted the text meant that it was not truly an instructional routine that allowed for the students to employ these practices to make meaning with texts. Instead, these notes tended to serve as moments for students to reproduce ideas that had previously been explicated by their teacher. In Mr. Gomez's class, students were rarely expected to silently and independently make meaning with books. Their primary role in the classroom reading was to listen to recitations and oral interpretations of the text. Moreover, on the occasions when they were called upon, they were expected to recite the text themselves.

Implications for Students Considered to be LTELs

As in the previous chapter, the commitment of Mr. Gomez and Mrs. Rodriguez to make information accessible to students is evident. This chapter builds upon the patterns identified in Chapter 3 about the nature of texts to illustrate that written texts were not the primary resource that students used to learn. The students were consistently presented with an oral recitation of the text as well as a teacher's interpretation of the meaning. Across all types of texts that comprised instructional reading events, group reading, meaning-making aloud, and teacher oral interpretation of the text were dominant practices. Although this chapter highlights official reading practices, this focus does not mean that Destiny, Eliza, Jamilet, Lizbeth, and Valeria adopted these reading practices when they engaged with texts individually or participated in the instructional reading events in the ways that their teachers desired. (Acknowledging this possibility of divergent ways of meaning-making, Chapter 5 examines the students' individual reading practices.) Nevertheless, these patterns play an integral role in providing a multidimensional representation of the focal students as readers and in contextualizing the focal students' performance on standardized assessments that were used to evaluate their English proficiency.

While the focal students and many of their classmates were considered to be LTELs and ELs, their teachers' instruction expressed confidence in the students' (oral) English language abilities. The centrality of spoken English across the observed classes and teacher and student reports about its significance in courses that I did not observe reinforces the extent of the students' oral English abilities. However, these practices also illustrated a belief that students would not and/

or could not read extended grade-level texts. This belief was reinforced by the absence of extended disciplinary texts and the dominant classroom reading comprehension practices. The teachers at New Millennium High School created an instructional environment that relied heavily on the students' (oral) English language proficiency. Specifically, they avoided presenting students with extended written discourse, and oral meaning-making in groups was the dominant reading comprehension practice.

Next Steps

Students who are considered to be LTELs need access to supported experiences to make meaning with diverse academic texts independently. While silent and independent reading may be intuitively relevant for many educators, it may not seem as pertinent to all students. Students like Destiny, Eliza, Jamilet, Lizbeth, and Valeria have been accustomed to listening to and engaging with oral recitations of text with the teacher providing an official interpretation for the majority of their educational trajectory. As a result, a quick change to more silent reading that is focused on independent comprehension may seem jarring and unnecessary. In my personal experience as a classroom teacher and in the classrooms that I have observed for research purposes, change in expectations for reading practices can result in resistance from students. Rather than talking about how to teach particular reading practices, this section addresses how to talk to young people about why reading silently and independently is a relevant reading practice. In order to create a classroom environment that is friendly to silent and independent meaning-making, it should be presented as an activity in which the students already successfully engage in other settings and which they are merely extending through instruction. Moreover, it should be identified as a practice that will be meaningful to their futures.

Successful Readers

One of the things that is accomplished by describing so-called LTELs as struggling readers in more than one language is that they are seen as not having any literacy abilities in either language. However, qualitative research that is critical of LTEL and other labels illustrates that this description of their abilities is not accurate (Brooks, 2017; de los Ríos, 2018; de los Ríos & Seltzer, 2017). Nevertheless, students can sometimes believe these misconceptions about themselves. Therefore, it is essential that there is a space within classroom literacy instruction to acknowledge students' existing literacy abilities as important in and of themselves and as relevant for future course-specific learning. This acknowledgement draws into what makes literacy instruction humanizing because it recognizes the multifaceted abilities of young people in the classroom. One pathway to achieve this goal is through having students identify how they are already reading in out-of-school spaces. Literacies that are not directly connected to school are sometimes seen as disconnected from academic contexts; however, these practices are sources of strength for student academic development (e.g., Hinchman, Alvermann, Boyd, Brozo, & Vacca, 2003; Kinloch et al., 2017; Kiramba, 2017; Karam, 2018; Skerrett, 2014).

One activity in which students can begin to consider what literacy practices they already engage in is to have them keep a diary of their activities over a particular weekend (see Table 4.3 for 24-hour diary template). After students bring this completed diary to school, ask them to think about the various types of texts they used during each of these activities. Remind students that these texts do not have to be English, they can include digital, visual, and other types of literacies, and do not have to be formally published. It helps to have models of bus schedules, screenshots of social media applications, advertisements, utility bills, and other examples of non-traditional texts. This way students can consider different types of texts that might not have initially been included in their understanding of text. The goal of the diary activity is to have them gather data about the ways in which they already are making meaning with texts for different purposes. Afterward,

TABLE 4.3 Weekend diary

Hours	Friday	Saturday	Sunday
12am–1am			
1am–2am			
2am–3am			
3am–4am			
4am–5am			
5am–6am			
6am–7am			
7am–8am			
8am–9am	School		
9am–10am	School		
10am–11am	School		
11am–12pm	School		
12pm–1pm	School		
1pm–2pm	School		
2pm–3pm	School		
3pm–4pm			
4pm–5pm			
5pm–6pm			
6pm–7pm			
7pm–8pm			
8pm–9pm			
9pm–10pm			
10pm–11pm			
11pm–12am			

they are able to consider how they read the texts and identify the distinct ways in which they read across the day. This provides a forum for educators and students to acknowledge students' existing literacy abilities. Moreover, it can be useful if students resist reading silently and independently because educators can remind youth about how they are already successful literacy users. Lastly, this information can also be helpful in making an argument for why silent reading is important because its relevance to everyday life has been made explicit.

Meaningful for Futures

Beyond reading silently and independently for the purposes of participating in class, it is necessary to consider how silent reading is used within the discipline and by those professions that are associated with the discipline. In other words, reading extended texts silently is not just about completing coursework. It is about expanding upon a reading practice that could provide access to new experiences in the world. In the context of English language arts, educators can draw connections between silent reading and the composing practices of different authors. In math and history, this includes exploring how mathematicians and historians can use silent and independent reading within the context of doing their work. However, it can also include connections between English language arts and Social Studies/History, such as the job of speech writers for politicians. The investigation could focus on how speech writers obtain the information they need to create a text that in the end becomes oral. In terms of science, it could include the work of scientists within a lab and journalists who communicate the connections between science and everyday life to the general populace. Across content areas, educators can show the connection to everyday professional settings that students might encounter. This instructional practice entails including references to the role that silent and independent reading plays in the lives of the professions with which they interact most closely or in which they have a desire to participate. It requires talking to students about where they see themselves in their immediate futures and incorporating this information into how the lesson is conducted.

Closing

Literacy education becomes humanizing when it recognizes the agency of students and is connected to the real world. This chapter builds upon the practices of care in which Mr. Gomez and Mrs. Rodriguez already engaged through their desire to make texts accessible and readily available to their students. Specifically, it provides a pathway for students to engage in their own independent meaning-making. Rather than relying on the assumption that students do not already engage in productive practices, this creates a space in which educators are able to draw on what students already know to make an argument for a movement toward new reading practices.

Notes

1 Portions of this chapter appeared previously in "'It's Like a Script': Long-Term English Learners' Experiences with and Ideas about Academic Reading." *Research in the Teaching of English, 49*(4), 383–406. Copyright © 2015 by the National Council of Teachers of English. Used with permission.

2 Brooks (2016) provides a more detailed examination of this practice focusing solely on Lizbeth's experiences of reading.

3 The notes in Figure 4.2 were taken from a specific class period because Mr. Gomez did not collect the reading notes from the class on which the vignette focused. The reading notes address a different scene in the book when Victor's dad leaves the house to go to a cantina and gets himself and his horse drunk.

5

CONSTRUCTING MEANING INDEPENDENTLY

An In-depth Analysis of Reading from an Individual Perspective[1]

> A good reader knows how to read and gets it and that they like if you ask them what was the book about they tell you everything.
>
> *Lizbeth Sanchez*

The previous chapters have examined the patterns in texts and classroom reading practices in Mrs. Rodriguez's biology and Mr. Gomez's English language arts classrooms. However, I have spent very little time so far discussing Destiny, Eliza, Jamilet, Lizbeth, and Valeria's independent reading practices. Solely because students experience certain ways of reading within their classrooms, it does not mean that this limits all that they know about reading and what they can do with texts. After all, students' literacy experiences extend beyond the classroom (Flores, 2018; O'Brien, Beach, & Scharber, 2007; Karam, 2018; Kiramba, 2017; Stewart, 2014). They engage in literate activity online, with video games, and with their families. Valeria was a student who had an active out-of-school literacy life in her evangelical church. As a member of a youth ministry group, she attended Bible study, created YouTube videos, and designed flyers. Moreover, students can reject the official reading practices of the learning setting. For example, Leo, a Spanish-English bilingual focal student in Frankel and Fields' (2019) research challenged the norms of reading and tutoring in the after-school reading clinic that he attended. His deviations from expected reading practices demonstrated the ways in which he was successful in reading and rejected certain types of reading practices that were institutionally positioned as valuable. In other words, adolescents have agency in their literacy practices and behaviors (Enriquez, 2011; Glenn & Ginsberg, 2016). Central to humanizing research and humanizing instruction is to explicitly understand how students are making meaning and engaging with literacy practices. This perspective that recognizes student agency and individuality is limited in much of the practitioner-focused work about students who are considered to be LTELs.

This chapter seeks to counter that tradition by not talking about LTELs as broad and general descriptions of students as struggling readers and failed learners of English. Rather than classroom reading practices, this description highlights individual reading practices of the five focal students. However, this focus on five individual teenage girls may bring up several questions about relevance to distinct classroom environments. These questions include, but are not limited to: How can this analysis be relevant for male students? These teenagers lived in a major urban area, what are the connections to rural contexts? The goal of this chapter is not to read the descriptions of Destiny, Eliza, Jamilet, Lizbeth, and Valeria's independent reading practices and assume that all LTEL students read and think about reading in the exact same ways. The purpose of the focus on the individual is to show what asking students about their ideas about reading and observing their reading practices revealed about their abilities. These lessons about seeing hidden abilities and identifying the impact of cumulative instructional experience can be taken into classrooms to further the creation of learning environments that recognize brilliance. This type of analysis contributes to educators' ability to avoid the fetishization of methods that Bartolomé (1994) argues is characteristic of dehumanizing literacy teaching.

In this chapter, I describe how Destiny, Eliza, Jamilet, Lizbeth, and Valeria talked about reading, in general, and how they talked about the specific practices they used when they independently read a biology and an English language arts text. Then, I situate these findings within their other experiences with classroom reading comprehension practices in their tenth-grade biology and English language arts courses. Throughout the chapter, I highlight ways in which educators can consider what kinds of opportunities to learn exist in their current classrooms or will exist in their future classrooms. Finally, I close the chapter illustrating how the gradual release of responsibility model can be used to teach strategies that can help students persist through texts that they find confusing and/or difficult.

Five Similar Perspectives on Reading

Learning about students' ideas about reading is important because existing research suggests that there is an interconnection between ideas about reading and reading practices (e.g., Alvermann et al., 1996; Barton, 2006; Hall, 2012, 2016; Kamhi-Stein, 2003; Mason, Scirica, & Salvi, 2006; Schraw, 2000). For example, Hall's (2016) research with an eighth-grade English language arts teacher shows that when a teacher recognizes students' ideas about reading it can impact pedagogy in critical ways. The classroom teacher in her research was able to integrate students' goals and understandings about reading with her own instructional goals. In this way, both teacher and students had some ownership over the curriculum. However, much of the research about LTELs and reading is predominated by reports of standardized test scores or assumptions about students' reading abilities based on these test scores. Students' ideas about reading cannot be garnered solely from standardized test scores. It is necessary to talk to the students themselves. Below, I share what I learned from talking to Destiny, Eliza, Jamilet, Lizbeth, and Valeria.

Interrelation of Experiences and Ideas about Reading

The focal students' current and historical experiences with reading were reflected in their ideas about reading, which they shared during interviews. The most frequently referenced characteristic of being a "good reader" related to what reading researchers describe as oral reading fluency. All of the focal students responded with some version of the following response:

1.   Good readers do not stumble over words, stutter, misread words, read in a low voice, or read slowly.

The second response that was shared among the focal students was the representation of reading comprehension as a passive and immediate process. This representation can be distilled into the following statement:

2.   Good readers immediately understand what they read.

The final response was mentioned by all of the students except Lizbeth. They noted a behavioral aspect to being a good reader. In summation, they articulated:

3.   Good readers behave like "good" students.

The focal students' ideas about reading centered on oral reading fluency, passive comprehension of texts, and demonstrating observable reading behaviors that are identified as those of a good student (e.g., engaging with text when asked to read and reading on a daily basis).

These conceptions of good reading reflected the valued practices that were described in Chapter 4. While the teenagers could list many criteria by which they could read aloud successfully or by which they could demonstrate "good student" behaviors, their responses about reading comprehension were less detailed. Comprehension was presented as something that either happened or did not happen. The focus on immediate comprehension in the second theme of good reading mirrored the dominant practice of reading aloud. When a text was read aloud and the teacher did not summarize it, if comprehension was not immediate then the opportunity to gather the information was lost—unless the listener asked a clarifying question of the teacher or someone sitting nearby.

This vision of text comprehension was illustrated in Lizbeth's response when she described a good reader as someone who "knows how to read and gets it and that they like if you ask them what was the book about they tell you everything ... what the book was about and that stuff." She described good readers as those who

Create an in-class activity where your students can share their ideas about what makes a successful reader in your subject area. Then, incorporate the information that you learn from your students into your instruction about reading in your subject matter. It is important to explicitly reference that you got these ideas and information from the students themselves.

- This activity does not have to be a traditional written assignment. Students can use the internet to gather images that represent the important reading practices.
- If they are stuck, asking students what makes someone an unsuccessful reader can be a pathway forward to complete the assignment.
- Take note of the common patterns among all students and among relevant subgroups.

FIGURE 5.1 Create change: Build upon students' ideas about reading

understood what they read immediately; therefore, not understanding meant that you were not a good reader. The focal students did not mention using comprehension strategies to make meaning with the text or the possibility of multiple interpretations of meaning. The students' talk about reading during the interviews suggested that they saw reading as a task that primarily consisted of oral reading fluency and immediate comprehension. The focal students saw comprehension as meaning that the reader was tasked with extracting the singular meaning from the text (Figure 5.1 provides guidance for learning about students' ideas about reading).

"Doing" Independent Reading

Like Borko and Eisenhart (1986, p. 588), I believed that "these understandings [of reading] might be related to their approaches to the task of reading." In order to better appreciate their relationship for Destiny, Eliza, Jamilet, Lizbeth, and Valeria, I designed a task in which each student had to think-aloud while reading a biology text and an English language arts text. Both texts were in English. These think-alouds provided detailed insight into the students' reading practices that was not available from their talk about reading or observing classroom reading practices (Smagorinsky, 2001b). Interestingly, the five girls engaged in diverse "active" reading practices during the think-alouds. Before I elaborate on what I learned from examining the students' think-alouds, I describe how they were conducted in more detail. First, I discuss the factors that influenced my selection of texts. Then, I explicitly share the nature of the interaction between the focal students and me during the think-alouds. This additional contextualization will situate the reading practices that I observed within the think-aloud activity.

Text Selection

My awareness of the focal students' negative feelings about in-class reading shaped my selection of texts for the think-alouds. Over the course of a year of observations, my concern about students not wanting to participate in the think-alouds was reinforced by witnessing and hearing about several instances of the focal students refusing to read. For example, Valeria's homeroom teacher explained to me that she had initially refused to take the state English language arts standardized test. She only continued with the exam after much coaxing on his part. When I asked Valeria why she did not want to read the texts, she explained that the passages were "too long," and they "made her tired." The perceived length of the text was a reoccurring factor that I witnessed influence several of the focal students' willingness to read.

I needed to select texts that were long enough to allow me to observe how students independently read extended multi-paragraph discourse. However, it could not be so long that it intimidated the students from participating in the think-aloud. In order to create a situation that would make the students more comfortable in participating in the think-alouds, I made sure that the first text was shorter than the second. Then, I changed the margins to ensure that each text could fit into the smallest number of pages. The first text that I selected to represent English language arts was an autobiographical short story; it was a page of single-spaced text consisting of 577 words. The second text was 795-word article about a genetic disease that occupied 1¾ single-spaced pages. At the end of each reading, there was a written prompt that asked students to respond to the question drawing on information from the text.

Another factor that was important in my text selection was that the topic of the texts mirrored similar themes discussed in their classrooms, but addressed unfamiliar topics. The first text was an autobiographical short story written by Jesus Colón (1961), a Nuyorican author. He describes an incident that took place at night in a New York City subway station. Colón examines how the pervasiveness of racism in his daily life impacted his interactions with a White woman. This autobiographical short story shares some characteristics in common with the books that they read in English language arts. However, it took place in an unfamiliar setting and historical context. The second text was an article from a user-generated website that Mrs. Rodriguez used as a resource for instruction. The article was about a genetic disease called "Hurler's syndrome" (Uno, 2011). Since the students had spent over a month of class time learning about genetic disease, they were familiar with the general topic. However, they did not specifically learn about Hurler's syndrome. The article described the symptoms, diagnosis, and treatment of Hurler's syndrome.

Student Discontent

Despite my attempts to mitigate the focal students' negative reactions to the prospect of doing think-alouds, my presentation of the idea of completing a think-aloud was met with annoyance and begrudging participation. During the initial think-aloud, Jamilet unequivocally let me know her feelings about the matter.

Maneka: Okay, so this one is going to be kind of different because it's about … remember how I am telling you that language inside and outside of school and then this part is about reading and stuff. [Jamilet rolls her eyes at me.] So, let me explain what it is … it's kind of…

Jamilet: So, I have to read now…

Maneka: Yeah.

Jamilet: Fail

Maneka: I know. I'm sorry. But, it is short. It is only one page. So, let me explain what it is. So, what you're going to do is I'm going to give this to you. [I show her the text the Colón short story.]

Jamilet: Nooo! That is not short.

Maneka: Okay. It's one page. [Jamilet rolls her eyes for a second time.]

Although none of the other students expressed their distaste for reading in the same manner as Jamilet, they clearly stated that they were not happy about this situation in ways that reflected their own personalities. Eyes were rolled, sighs were emitted, and I was the target of whining teenagers. Nevertheless, all of the five teenagers participated in the think-aloud task.

Think-Aloud Instructions

During a practice session, I had students practice thinking aloud while completing a word search. Prior to giving each student the first text, I explained to the students that I wanted them to share their thoughts aloud as they read. During the think-alouds, my most frequent interactions with the students were procedural: student requests for clarification of instructions or my requests that they speak louder. When students would explicitly ask for assistance in interpreting the meaning of texts, I did not provide them with an answer. However, I encouraged them to share their thoughts with me. In this way, my interactions with the students were designed to reinforce the previously stated goals of understanding their independent reading practices. However, I also engaged in "cheerleading" interactions with the students. In these think-alouds, I had to give students explicit encouragement about the fact that they could, indeed, read the text. I did not tell them what or how they should read it. I did not share my thoughts about the meaning of the text.

Independent Reading in Action

Four categories of reading practices emerged from the previously described analysis: summarizing and identifying important information; making connections to background knowledge; going beyond the text; and recognizing limitations. Table 5.1 illustrates which girl used which practices. Below, in illustrating how the students demonstrate each practice. I provide an explanation of the practice.

TABLE 5.1 Categories of individual reading practices in which students engaged (from grouping emergent process codes)

Reading Practices	Destiny	Eliza	Jamilet	Lizbeth	Valeria
Summarizing and Identifying Important Information					
Summarizing	Both	Both	Both	Both	Both
Identifying Information	Both	Both	Both	Both	Both
Making Connections to Background Knowledge					
Connecting to Personal Life	Not Vocalized	Both	Biology	ELA	Both
Connecting to Content	Biology	Biology	Biology	Not Vocalized	Not Vocalized
Going Beyond the Text					
Giving Opinion	Not Vocalized	ELA	ELA	ELA	Not Vocalized
Making an Inference	ELA	ELA	ELA	ELA	Both
Recognizing Limitations					
Verbalizing Difficulty with Comprehension	Not Vocalized	Biology	Biology	Not Vocalized	Not Vocalized
Asking Questions (Self)	Not Vocalized	Both	Biology	Not Vocalized	Not Vocalized
Requesting Assistance	Not Vocalized	Both	Biology	Not Vocalized	Biology

Note. Both indicates that a participant engaged in this practice with both texts.
Biology represents that the student engaged in this practice with the Hurler's syndrome article.
ELA represents that the student engaged in this practice with the Colón short story.
Not Vocalized indicates that a participant did not vocalize this practice with either text.

Summarizing and Identifying Important Information. There were two reading practices that each girl vocalized across both texts: identifying important information and summarizing sections of text. Each student's ability to engage in these two reading practices with both texts is noteworthy. Recognizing important information and synthesizing a segment of text are essential reading practices in multiple content areas. Moreover, by summarizing and identifying important information, participants demonstrated the extent of particular aspects of their text comprehension.

Identifying important information was reflected in the students listing "facts" from the text. Table 5.2 illustrates how Valeria engaged identifying information

TABLE 5.2 Valeria's identification of important information

Valeria's vocalizations	Hurler's syndrome article (Uno, 2011, para. 4)
Okay. And uh … the disease uh … it's divided into three subtypes and *[reads quietly to herself for 11 seconds]* Okay and, um, this disease was identified in 19 … 9… 19 …1919 by a doctor and *[reads quietly to herself for 13 seconds]* and then … and the child also inherits the defective gen … gene from both parents which is mom and dad.	Hurler's syndrome is also called mucopolysaccharidoses type I (MPS I), Hurler's disease, and gargoylism. It belongs to a class of diseases called mucopolysaccharidoses or MPS. MPS1 is divided into three subtypes, based on severity of symptoms, the most severe being Hurler's syndrome. MPS1 S (Scheie syndrome) and MPS1 H-S (Hurler-Scheie syndrome) are the 2 other types. Hurler's syndrome was identified in 1919 by Dr. Gertrud Hurler. This syndrome occurs in 1 in every 100,000 births. The child inherits the defective gene from both parents. The parents may have one copy of the gene, but the child inherits two and hence this syndrome occurs.

while reading about Hurler's syndrome. In her vocalizations, she listed bits of information that she had determined to be significant. For example, she repeated the year the disease was discovered and described how it is inherited. In contrast, summarizing sections of text requires that the student not only identify key information, but also produce and vocalize a synthesis of this information. For example, Lizbeth demonstrated this ability when she summarized the last paragraph of the Hurler's syndrome article (see Table 5.3). She drew on information in the written text to provide an overview of its meaning.

As described above, the students' identification of key information and summaries illustrated depth of comprehension; however, they also indicated student misconceptions about the text. The misunderstandings that the students demonstrated while reading Colón's short story were superficial and unimportant to interpreting the global meaning of the text. Throughout the entire reading, Destiny and Lizbeth incorrectly identified the narrator as a woman. In the case of the Hurler's syndrome article, there was more confusion about the actual content of the text. These difficulties illustrated misunderstandings about specific word meanings that reflected broader conceptual relationships. For example, Jamilet had difficulty distinguishing the terms and the relationships between *syndrome*, *symptom*, and *disease*. Similarly, Eliza expressed confusion about the relationship between *disorder* and *syndrome*. Valeria avoided these terms in her explanations by referring to all of them as a "sickness." Unlike the students' difficulties with discerning whether the narrator was male or female, Eliza, Jamilet, and Valeria's

TABLE 5.3 Lizbeth's summary of text section

Lizbeth's vocalizations	*Hurler's syndrome article (Uno, 2011, para. 9)*
This one says that there should be a lot of specialists involved with the treatment because there are lots of parts of the body that are affected.	Due to different areas that are affected by this disorder, a variety of specialists must be involved in the care and treatment. Limiting intake of sugar and milk products helps in reducing mucus levels. Physical therapy helps in easing some of the pain associated with joint problems. But each case of Hurler's syndrome is unique and highly individual, so orthopedics and physical therapists must be consulted for guidance.

particular vocabulary trouble could impede a more comprehensive understanding of the genetic disease detailed in the article.

Connecting to Background Knowledge. Connecting the content of the texts to background knowledge was another reading practice that occurred across both texts. This practice is frequently identified as one of the many ways successful readers make meaning with texts (e.g., Duke & Pearson, 2009). There were two ways in which students engaged in these practices—making connections with their personal life and making connections to content area knowledge. When students made connections to their personal life, they drew on resources that were not explicitly related to their previous instructional experiences to comprehend a text. When relying on content knowledge, they drew on their previous in-school instructional experiences in the classes I observed or they explicitly referenced instruction. In order to engage in either one of these practices, each participant needed sufficient understanding of the text to find and make an appropriate connection to her background knowledge. These explicit allusions to personal and instructional background knowledge implied substantive comprehension of the texts they read.

While reading Colón's short story, Eliza, Valeria, and Lizbeth shared stories that related this text to a personal experience. For example, Eliza, who is a very fair-skinned Latina with green eyes and dyed red hair, shared an experience that was analogous to Colón's fear of being discriminated against. Her shared experience mirrored the two levels of discrimination that Colón fears: ethnic origin and skin color.

> **Eliza:** Yeah. I know. I get that a lot because I am ... well not because I am ... every time I am near Caucasian people and I am with my cousins and they are like darker than me. So, it is weird because we like try to help people and we always like, oh, I mean that they don't feel comfortable with

it ... There's this one situation where an old lady. I don't know, we were over by Sunset and this old lady she was like putting ... she was like taking things out of her car and they were like big heavy things. So, he was like. He was like, "I don't know if I should ask her or not." And then, one of my cousins did and she was like, "I don't need your help." Yeah, so. I was like, "Wow. You're heartless."

Eliza's anecdote connects to Colón's specific discussion of his fears of being a Puerto Rican man of African descent approaching a White woman on a subway platform. Her story recognizes that although she and her cousins may share an identification with the Latino ethnic categorization, the ways in which their phenotypes are racialized present unique concerns for their unequal treatment. She explicitly acknowledged how her cousins' darker skin color influenced their interaction with the older stranger, demonstrating that Eliza understood this nuanced aspect of the short story. In addition, Eliza, Jamilet, and Valeria made personal connections with the Hurler's syndrome article.

The practice of relating texts to prior instructional content knowledge only occurred during the transcripts of the think-alouds for the Hurler's syndrome article. This was an interesting phenomenon, considering the fact that both texts related to themes that all participants had previously encountered in academic courses. While reading the article about Hurler's syndrome, Destiny, Eliza, and Jamilet drew explicitly on previous biology content knowledge to interpret the text. They identified subject matter that had been part of the instruction they had received in Mrs. Rodriguez's biology class (sometimes explicitly referring to Mrs. Rodriguez by name). For example, Destiny commented, "So ... this is like what Mrs. Rodriguez taught us about the enzymes." Beyond these concrete references to instruction, the influence of their previous instruction was also reflected in what participants did and did not vocalize. For example, their summaries and identification of key information focused on areas of prior in-class instruction, such as how genetic diseases are inherited.

Going Beyond the Text. Each student made inferences when reading Colón's short story. In other words, they took information that was present in the text and used it to make a conjecture about information that was not explicitly stated. For instance, after reading the description of the woman on the subway, Destiny commented: "So this lady must be a single mother because she is only with her kids and then she is carrying a suitcase." Destiny used the description provided by Colón to make inferences about the character's background. Making an inference requires that students understand the plot and are able to build a hypothesis that is connected to the story. Only one student, Valeria, made inferences about the science text. She inferred what was happening in the house of a sick child, which she imagined the text was describing. She created a background story of the experience of a fictional family, who has a child with Hurler's syndrome. These inferences were based on her comprehension of the text and her personal experience of having a brother with special needs. The inferences that students made involved drawing connections between their personal life experiences and the texts. None of the girls used explicitly school-based information, such as information they studied about genetic diseases, to make inferences about either text.

The transcripts of Jamilet's, Lizbeth's, and Eliza's think-aloud protocols about Colón's short story represented a way of moving beyond the text that was distinct from the other two students. While thinking-aloud, these three teenagers shared their opinion about Colón's actions and behaviors—both as an author and as the main character of the text. For example, Lizbeth shared an insight into a pivotal moment in Colón's autobiographical short story. In addition to explaining that Colón regrets his decision not to be courteous, she interjected her own opinion: "In this one, I think that she should feel badly because she didn't help the lady and she should have manners and like help her with something at least." Lizbeth vocalized her perspective, referencing Colón as she, and gave her opinion authoritatively in the meaning-making process. Destiny and Valeria tended to treat the text as a repository of information from which their goal was to extract information. In contrast, Jamilet's, Lizbeth's, and Eliza's interactions with and responses to Colón's text demonstrated a distinct collaborative relationship with the text. This way of interacting with the short story reflected a conception of comprehension that is actively constructed by the reader, rather than being transmitted from the text.

Recognizing Limitations. The final three reading practices that emerged from the transcripts illustrate Eliza, Jamilet, and Valeria's abilities to recognize their own limitations in comprehending a particular aspect of the text through verbalizing difficulty with comprehension, asking a self-directed question, or requesting assistance from me. This recognition of their own limitations in understanding a text segment illustrates that these three participants were monitoring their own comprehension, a practice that is identified in the research literature as one way

---

Ask students to bring a text to class that makes them feel like successful readers. Then, ask students to explain to the class how to read the particular text.

- It helps to bring examples of nontraditional texts (e.g., video game instructions, train schedules, music lyrics, and social media transcripts) and texts in languages other than English.
- Modeling thinking aloud with an out-of-school text from your personal life is necessary to show students how to demonstrate their thinking.
- Consider having students practice modeling their thinking in pairs before sharing with the class.
- As students are sharing, write down one productive practice that each student demonstrates. Later, you can specifically reference a student's successful practice and connect it back to a relevant disciplinary literacy practice.

FIGURE 5.2 Create change: Build upon student success

that successful comprehenders engage with making meaning (see Duke & Pearson, 2009). Moreover, this group of reading practices provides another forum to illustrate the extent to which Eliza, Jamilet, and Valeria understood the text.

For the first of the three reading practices—verbalizing difficulty with comprehension—Jamilet and Eliza expressed an inability to understand a segment of the Hurler's syndrome article. They articulated a nuanced identification of the specific parts of the text that were causing them difficulty. For example, while pointing at the bullet-pointed list of symptoms, Jamilet shared: "I have no idea what they are." However, she did not continue to try to find a way to make sense of the list. Instead, she acknowledged that she did not understand the text segment and moved on to the next paragraph. Jamilet, Eliza and Valeria also relied on question-asking to gain a better understanding of the text. In this context, these questions were used to seek clarity. However, the question-asking practices had different audiences. The audience for the first type of question-asking practice was the teenager herself. Jamilet vocalized this practice only with the Hurler's syndrome article; on the other hand, Eliza employed self-directed questions while reading both texts. During the second type of question-asking reading practice, which Eliza, Jamilet, and Valeria employed, they were expecting a response from me. I did not respond to their questions but instead asked them what they thought. Eliza engaged in this type of question-asking practice with both texts. However, Jamilet and Valeria only asked me these types of question about the Hurler's syndrome article.

The three ways of recognizing limitations suggest that the participants were aware of an area of their own limited comprehension. The two forms of question-asking were both aimed at obtaining more information to continue making meaning with the text. The former strategy requires a student to look into the text and within her own background knowledge for assistance, whereas the latter strategy orients the student to a perceived more knowledgeable authority figure for an answer. Through these previously described reading practices Jamilet, Eliza, and Valeria recognized their own limitations, yet they did not vocalize multiple ways to repair comprehension.

Reading Strategies in the Classroom

Throughout the two think-aloud protocols, Destiny, Eliza, Jamilet, Lizbeth, and Valeria engaged in a variety of reading practices to independently make meaning. I organized their reading practices into four categories: summarizing and identifying important information; making connections to background knowledge; going beyond the text; and recognizing limitations. These reading practices provide evidence that these teenagers were actively making meaning with the texts. Not only were they engaging in reading practices that the reading comprehension literature values, this analysis highlighted the detailed nature of their text comprehension. Their ways of actively reading differed from what they verbalized was important about reading. It also highlighted areas of difficulty. Destiny, Eliza,

Lizbeth, Jamilet, and Valeria appeared to be inexperienced in how to approach unfamiliar content. Eliza, Jamilet, and Valeria were able to verbally recognize the fact that they did not understand a particular section or word, but did not demonstrate multiple ways of addressing these areas of confusion. These findings suggest that the five focal students are inexperienced with specific reading practices that would facilitate making sense of texts whose content is unfamiliar.

Engagement with Unfamiliar Content

The students' inexperience with specific types of meaning-making practices contrasted with the presence of strategy instruction that I witnessed during my classroom observations. Strategy instruction was integrated into Mr. Gomez's English curriculum and, to a lesser extent, Mrs. Rodriguez's biology class. As described in Chapter 4, Mr. Gomez's explicit strategy instruction took the form of the daily implementation of reading notes, which were informed by the Seven Habits of Effective Readers. During the think-alouds, all of the students employed several of the seven "habits," which were an integral part of their English language arts instructional experiences (see Table 5.4). In Mrs. Rodriguez's class, strategic reading instruction was limited to the rare instances when students were reading extended multi-paragraph texts written by distant authors. Yet, other than Eliza, Jamilet, and Valeria "asking questions," the students did not attempt to use any of the strategies that they were taught to address difficulties with comprehension.

The presence of reading practices that could be used to construct meaning with texts that contain unfamiliar content in their instruction and in their individual reading repertoire, raises an significant question: If the focal students could employ these practices and they were receiving instruction about their significance, why did they not use them in think-alouds when confronted with unfamiliar content? In response to this question, it is necessary to point out that Destiny, Eliza, Jamilet, Lizbeth and Valeria did not have frequent opportunities to use these strategies to independently make meaning with unfamiliar texts.

In order to illustrate how strategy instruction can occur without using them to make meaning, I return to Mr. Gomez's use of the Seven Habits of Effective Readers

TABLE 5.4 Seven Habits of Effective Readers

Strategy	Mr. Gomez's Definition
Make Meaning	Identify something you don't understand
Question	Ask a question
Visualize	Draw physically (paint a mental picture)
Determine Importance	Identify an important quote
Activate Schema	Make connections to prior knowledge
Synthesize	Write a summary
Drawing Inferences	Make a prediction

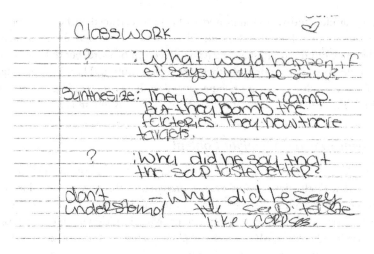

FIGURE 5.3 Destiny's "effective" reading notes

and the corresponding reading notes that Destiny (see Figure 5.3) composed as the class read the book *Night* (Wiesel & Wiesel, 2006). Destiny provides evidence in notes that she engaged in the effective reading habits required by Mr. Gomez. However, it is important to look at the purpose these notes served within the classroom. These notes were used as evidence that she was listening to the reading, rather than as a way to practice using the "habits" to make sense of a confusing text.

In this excerpt of notes, the use of question-asking clearly illustrates the role of this reading strategy. Destiny employs the question-asking habit of effective reader three times: "What would happen if eli says what he saw?" "Why did he say that the soup taste better?" "Why did he say the soup taste like corpses." By writing down these questions, Destiny indicates that she understands the content of the story being read to her. However, she does not have the opportunity to explicitly return to the text to answer these questions. These questions were not an opportunity to use this "effective reading habit" to correct misunderstandings or to facilitate comprehension. The strategy is already considered to have been successfully employed when the question is merely asked. In many ways, the reading practices in which students engaged in the think-alouds mirrored the practices to which they had become accustomed in their English language arts classroom. They were ways to illustrate "effective reading," but not necessarily ways of constructing meaning when confronted with unfamiliar content.

Although Mrs. Rodriguez and Mr. Gomez focused on reading strategy instruction, the focal students did not have many in-class opportunities to use these reading practices independently with texts containing unfamiliar content. There are two factors to which I attribute these limited opportunities. The first factor relates to the frequency and construction of teacher-assembled texts. In Chapter 3, I discussed the fact that teacher-assembled texts were tailored specifically to the personal background knowledge of the students in the classroom. In other words,

Create a video compilation of soon-to-be graduating students, teachers, administrators, alumni, and other people at school or in the community talking about when they experience difficulty with reading and how they cope with this difficulty.

- Remember to include people of a variety of ages, language backgrounds, genders, and race/ethnicities.
- This type of video normalizes the fact that everyone experiences difficulty at some point.
- Talk to students about what surprised them about other people's difficulties and their responses to these difficulties.
- Explicitly incorporate instruction about what to do when you encounter difficulty with particular types of texts.

FIGURE 5.4 Create change: Normalize difficulty

these five young people were unaccustomed to encountering texts that contained large amounts of unfamiliar information. The second factor relates to the nature of classroom reading practices. When students were presented with texts that did contain unfamiliar content, they were rarely expected to make meaning individually. Since most reading took place aloud and in a group, the teacher or another more knowledgeable individual was usually present to interpret the text and to provide the missing connections for any student who was confused. This practice was also evident in Chapter 4. During classroom instruction, the focal students did not encounter completely unfamiliar information without the support of another, more knowledgeable, individual.

The reading situation that they confronted in the think-alouds was uncommon. They were precluded from relying on the most frequent strategy that they used for accessing unknown information in a text: asking another person for the "official" meaning of a text. This reading practice was attempted by Eliza, Jamilet, and Valeria in their think-alouds. As a result, I contend that the five students' individual reading practices reflected their dominant experiences with in-class reading (see Figure 5.4 for a multimedia activity on normalizing reading difficulties).

Implications for Students Considered to be LTELs

Independent meaning-making with extended texts was an infrequent classroom practice. Nevertheless, I dedicated this chapter to focusing on this topic because this way of engaging with texts plays an integral role in the focal students' educational trajectory. Based on my interviews with Destiny, Eliza, Jamilet, Lizbeth, and Valeria, it appeared that they held beliefs about comprehension as extracting a singular meaning from the text. These ways of talking about reading reflected the predominant beliefs held by "struggling readers" in the existing reading research literature (Frankel & Fields, 2019; Hall, 2016; Menken & Kleyn, 2010). Moreover, they reflected their current and historical experiences with in-school reading. They highlighted oral reading fluency, immediate and passive comprehension of the text, and behavioral aspects of reading. When they were explicitly asked to place meaning-making before the "fluent" oral realization of the texts, each teenager demonstrated the ability to engage in multiple reading practices that the reading comprehension literature has identified as characteristic of proficient readers (e.g., Pressley & Afflerbach, 1995).

These five teenagers demonstrated these meaning-making practices in varied ways with extended multi-paragraph texts that were written by a "distant" author and in a context in which they were expected to read silently and independently. These think-alouds demonstrated that there was a difference between what the focal students said made a successful reader and what they were able to do with texts. Although the students employed multiple "active" reading practices while making meaning with the two selected texts, they did not use these multiple reading practices to clarify areas of confusion within the text. Their day-to-day classroom reading experiences did not provide them with many opportunities to do so.

Students were inexperienced in employing these reading practices to make meaning with unfamiliar content and text types. These difficulties are not unique to ELs, but reflect their experiences with these reading comprehension practices during classroom instruction. When the focus is solely on positioning students as "long-term" learners of English, it can prevent literacy educators from recognizing how they are successful readers and the best ways to construct supportive literacy learning environments. Moreover, it overlooks the fact that much of their struggle was not unique to their official classification as (long-term) English learners. As Chapter 4 illustrated, it was their oral English abilities that teachers relied on to communicate key content area information to students.

Next Steps

In order to have access to a variety of educational and career opportunities, students must be able to construct meaning from diverse texts independently. However, the transition from relying on the teacher "giving" students the meaning of a text to the students constructing meaning independently can be difficult. In my own experience as both a teacher and researcher, I have seen adolescents that are accustomed to being read to resist this change. Furthermore, I have shared the fears of teachers who worry that students will not be able to construct meaning from academic texts independently. However, Pearson and Gallagher's (1983) Gradual Release of Responsibility Model provides a way to support students in gaining multiple experiences with constructing meaning independently. This model is especially relevant to the kind of instructional context that I described in this chapter because it builds on teachers' desire to ensure that students have access to content, while transitioning students to engage in the desired independent reading practices.

Duke, Pearson, Strachan, and Billman (2011) draw on the previous work of Duke and Pearson (2002) to outline how this model functions with the teaching of strategies for reading comprehension. The strategies that are the focus of instruction are usually drawn from research that has identified what successful readers actually do when they engage in making meaning with texts. Various research and practitioner-oriented texts highlight numerous strategies as being effective. For example, the Seven Habits of Effective Readers employed by Mr. Gomez illustrate some of these frequently used strategies. However, this list focuses on some of the more general strategies that have been criticized by some researchers and practitioners for overlooking the uniqueness of reading in various disciplines (Shanahan & Shanahan, 2008, 2012). In their 2012 article, Shanahan and Shanahan (p. 11) provide an example of how reading can differ across disciplines:

> Although historians and history students must consider a text's authorial source to understand context, research has revealed a different pattern of reading for scientists (Shanahan et al., 2011). Our interviews with chemists have shown that they do rely on author but more as a topical or quality screen when determining which texts to read … Once reading begins, unlike the historians, however, scientists try to focus their attention specifically on the text.

Taking these disciplinary differences into account is pedagogically meaningful; however, I argue that it is important for teachers to also consider both general reading practices and those that are desired in the discipline. For students who are experiencing difficulties with reading, these research-based general strategies may be necessary to provide access to disciplinary texts (Faggella-Luby, Sampson Graner, Deshler, & Valentino Drew, 2012). However, literacy instruction should not be limited to providing access to content area knowledge; it should include opportunities for deeper disciplinary engagement.

The Gradual Release of Responsibility Model provides teachers with a framework to guide students in engaging with texts, rather than deciphering the text for them. Although Destiny, Eliza, Jamilet, Lizbeth, and Valeria's English language arts class introduced them to strategic reading, the way in which this was implemented was not to make meaning independently, but rather to demonstrate that they were attending to the teacher's explanations of the reading. The five stages of this model allow for teachers to gradually release the responsibility for comprehending texts to the students.

Duke et al. (2011, pp. 64–66) outline five stages with accompanying language to illustrate the kind of *teacher talk* that could occur within each of these stages: (1) an explicit description of the strategy and when and how it should be used; (2) teacher and/or student modeling of the strategy in action; (3) collaborative use of the strategy in action; (4) guided practice using the strategy with gradual release of responsibility; (5) independent use of the strategy. All of these stages do not necessarily need to take place during the same class period. In fact, the teacher must be acutely aware of the appropriate timing of these steps. S/he must maintain a balance between rushing through stages and refusing to *release* the responsibility for comprehension. Like scaffolding on a building under construction, the goal of this approach to instruction is to eventually remove the extra support and allow the students stand without assistance.

Duke et al. (2011) highlight that this approach to instruction is not merely following a series of linear steps. They note that the mere inclusion of each stage in an instruction routine will not ensure that students will know how to use the strategy independently. Instead, the authors describe the importance of the recursive nature of this framework. Duke et al. acknowledge that students may forget about a strategy or struggle to apply it in a new situation. Second, the authors emphasize that it is important for teachers to recognize that students will not need to use the same strategy daily. They differentiate between the necessity for periodic review and the way in which strategy instruction can lose its focus and become an instructional routine itself. The advantage of the Gradual Release of Responsibility Model is that it provides a framework for teachers to guide students in developing the desired strategic reading practices. Nevertheless, this way of engaging in literacy pedagogy does not need to be limited to strategy instruction. This model can be integrated into other areas of literacy and content area learning (see Fisher & Frey, 2014 for a practical guide to the possibilities of this model). The Gradual Release of Responsibility Model provides students with structured opportunity to learn the reading practices that are optimal for academic success. This pedagogical approach goes beyond exposure to content and pushes students towards deeper engagement in disciplinary learning.

Closing

Descriptions of LTELs that focus solely on their purported limited literacy abilities and ongoing "failure" to learn English flatten the multifaceted nature of their literacy abilities. This analysis of the individual reading practices shines light on the inaccuracy of broad descriptions of students. It calls attention to the necessity for a humanizing reading pedagogy to be inclusive of the strengths of students and to expand opportunities to learn. Importantly, the gradual release of responsibility model provides a framework towards moving to an even more student-centered classroom. It lays the basis to create space for students to continue their journey as agentive meaning-makers. This chapter's contribution towards humanizing education is through creating a space for students who are labeled LTELs to be seen as individuals within an educational context that presents them as monolithic.

Note

1 Portions of this chapter appeared previously in "'It's Like a Script': Long-Term English Learners' Experiences with and Ideas about Academic Reading." *Research in the Teaching of English*, 49(4), 383–406. Copyright © 2015 by the National Council of Teachers of English. Used with permission. Portions of this chapter appeared previously in "Tell me what you are thinking": An investigation of five Latina LTELs constructing meaning with academic texts. *Linguistics and Education*, 35, 1–14. Copyright © 2016 by Elsevier. Used with permission.

6

RECOGNIZING BRILLIANCE IN THE UNDERVALUED

Transforming Literacy Education for Long-term English Learners

> I don't think these kids will ever learn to speak English properly.
>
> *Anonymous*

Ricardo, a student in Mrs. Rodriguez's first-period class, who was also considered to be a long-term English learner, asked Ms. Rodriguez: "How come you didn't give me a bubble bath?" Surprised at the nature of the question, she looked at him, looked at me, and then looked back at him. I quickly interjected, "He meant bubble bath soap." Relieved, she laughed and said: "Oh, okay." Fortunately, I had already shared with Mrs. Rodriguez that during her absence the substitute teacher held a raffle for students who completed their work; one of the prizes was a bottle of bubble bath soap. Ricardo initially did not recognize the reason for the awkward silence and multiple looks, but after a few moments, it clicked. His face reddened and he said, "Oh! No! Miss! Soap!" We all laughed and class continued as usual.

Later that day, Mrs. Rodriguez and I were discussing the miscommunication in the main office when a visitor from a prestigious research university inserted his unsolicited comment into our conversation. He quipped, "I don't think these kids will ever learn to speak English properly." I didn't respond to his comment, excused myself, and stepped into an empty classroom where I searched for the meaning of "bubble bath" in an online dictionary. Even through this narrow prescriptivist arbiter of meaning, the dictionary, Ricardo's use of bubble bath was "proper." There are two definitions of bubble bath. The first definition refers to the "crystal powder or liquid preparation" and the second to the bath that contains this powder or preparation.

Perhaps the failure of the initial communication should rest on the shoulders of Mrs. Rodriguez for not immediately recognizing the multiple meanings of this term. On the other hand, one could argue that Ricardo should have considered the possibility that this term's multiple meanings could confuse a conversation partner. Regardless of the cause of the miscommunication, it took on new significance in this conversation in the office. It became evidence of the "limited English proficiency" of "these kids." This interaction in the office also highlighted the special burden that bilinguals, particularly those bilinguals who are from racially minoritized groups, carry; they are linguistically "suspicious." Any divergence from the standard monolingual norm or any misunderstanding can call their language proficiency into question.

Although the previously described incident involving Ricardo focused on oral language, I contend that the same suspicion underlies the prevalent interpretation of the low reading test scores of students labeled long-term English learners in educational research, policy, and practice. When these students do not meet expected benchmarks on standardized assessments of literacy in English, their failure to meet these goals is attributed to their "limited English proficiency." Olsen's (2010, p. 22) attempt to illustrate the differences between LTELs and monolingual English-speaking students who do not perform well on standardized tests of literacy is an excellent example of this phenomenon. She writes:

> Thus, their California Standards Test (CST) scores might look similar to struggling adolescent native speakers, and they also struggle with academic language and comprehending academic texts. Yet they are still English Learners—with gaps in the basic foundation of the English language. They share much in common with other Standard English Learner groups—the mix of English vocabulary superimposed on the structure of their heritage language, and the use of a dialect of English that differs from academic English. Yet they are still acquiring basic English syntax, grammar, structures and vocabulary that native English speakers have by virtue of growing up in homes where English was the spoken language.

The *privilege* of English monolingualism is evident in the previous excerpt. That is, growing up in a home where English is "the spoken language," regardless of the variety, confers certain inalienable linguistic abilities on the speaker. However, being raised in a home where English is only one of the languages spoken permits Olsen to attribute the source of their low standardized test scores to English proficiency without further investigation. This phenomenon is not unique to Olsen, but characterizes much of the research on English-speaking bilinguals, who are identified as LTELs, and has been documented in other contexts involving individuals from bilingual backgrounds.

For students who are considered to be LTELs, it is more than their bilingual backgrounds and racial positioning that permits their reading practices to be immediately attributed to their English proficiency level. Many publications on this population focus on *English learner*, and its more recent counterpart, *long-term English learner*, as the analytic lenses for teaching. These English proficiency classifications are treated as though they are neutral and objective linguistic descriptions of bilingual students' English competency. However, such classifications are not neutral, but are actually socially constructed policy categories. As exemplified in the work of Valdés, Poza, & Brooks (2015) about the LTEL classification and Kibler and Valdés (2016) about language learner categories broadly, these categories are situated within a particular sociocultural context in which they "reify existing popular and scholarly understandings and beliefs about what it means to learn or know a language" (Valdés et al., 2015). For example, the EL category is situated within "popular and scholarly" understandings, which identify specific kinds of literacy practices as being part of English proficiency *only* for bilingual students. These policy categories not only reside in the halls of the various legislatures that enacted them, but these categories and their respective conceptualizations of language and language learning are also integrated into educational practice. Therefore, they have a critical influence on bilingual students' educational trajectory.

Rejecting the LTEL label and the coinciding interpretations of the students to whom it is applied does not mean ignoring the reality of their classification. In fact, with students classified as ELs, educators have a legal and moral responsibility to consider both their linguistic and academic development. Moreover, ignoring the fact that students have remained in the EL classification for several years would be refusing to understand an essential part of their educational experiences. Rejecting the LTEL classification means that the number of years that a student has been classified as an EL is not a proxy for their linguistic experiences. In addition, it requires the recognition that reading is a multifaceted social practice and not just a modality of language. This perspective provides educators with a nuanced lens to consider what students' reading experiences and practices reveal about their abilities. In other words, it creates a pathway for creating academic environments to support the robust types of reading practices in which students should engage. The focus on creating a supportive literacy learning environment moves away from supposed deficiencies within students and attends to the pedagogical context.

A Focus on Opportunity to Learn

This multifaceted examination of Destiny, Eliza, Lizbeth, Jamilet, and Valeria's experiences suggests that their difficulties with reading are not uniquely due to their classification as ELs. During the think-alouds, which created a "safe" space in which they were encouraged to focus on comprehension, rather than on oral reading fluency, they demonstrated that they were not the elementary readers experiencing problems with decoding and basic comprehension who have been described in the research literature. Despite their low standardized reading test scores, they demonstrated the kind of active reading practices that the reading comprehension literature prizes. This does not mean, however, that they did not encounter areas of difficulty with these texts. Nevertheless, they were reading in ways that the research literature, their test scores, and even their classroom teachers overlooked. The representation of "long-term English learners" in this book is significant because it is infrequent within the discourse in educational research, policy, and practice.

Another major contribution of this book is that it calls attention to the focal students' in-school instructional experiences with reading. Specifically, it highlights the disconnect between their daily experiences with reading and standardized assessments. The students in the classrooms that I observed were being read to and receiving oral explanations of texts, most of which were written by the teachers. In their classrooms, reading was a group activity that occurred primarily with abbreviated teacher-assembled text, in which oral English was central to the meaning-making process. However, on standardized tests, students were expected to silently and independently construct meaning from extended texts written by distant authors. These ways of reading created distinct roles for the focal students as readers. In class, they were most often asked to listen to oral English that was connected to the written discourse of a text. Their role as readers, in this case, appears to be that of passive recipients of the "officially sanctioned" meaning as interpreted by the teacher. In contrast, on standardized tests, they were asked to arrive at an "officially sanctioned" meaning independently and silently. These are two distinct ideas about and activities of reading. Rather than "English," this research focuses attention on the instructional environment that students experience in elementary and secondary school.

If the goal of our educational system is to create students who are able to independently construct meaning from texts written by distant authors, then their classroom experiences must offer a variety of opportunities to engage in these practices. However, the absence of these kinds of instructional spaces cannot be placed solely on the teacher because it ignores the larger sociocultural circumstances in which these students have been educated. As students who began their education in schools during the implementation of Reading First,[1] they came to high school with a focus on fluency. They were accustomed to reading aloud as being the way that reading is done. When I saw the teachers attempting to change this practice, they encountered resistance from the students. All of the teachers with whom I spoke understood the importance of reading for their content area as well as in the students' post-secondary lives. However, they did not feel comfortable explicitly teaching reading—either because they were unfamiliar with reading pedagogy and/or they felt that they were constrained by mandates to cover specific subject content for standardized tests. The instructional practices in which teachers engaged reflected coping strategies for accomplishing the multiple demands that they encountered.

Reading Pedagogy: A Humanizing and Socially Informed Perspective

A humanizing and socially informed reading pedagogy is built on the recognition of English-speaking bilinguals' multifaceted linguistic abilities, regardless of their ongoing classification as English learners. The first step—as described above—would entail pushing back on using the LTEL/EL lens as an interpretive lens for reading education. This does not mean ignoring the fact that students are bilingual and their bilingualism in certain situations will provide unique affordances or difficulties. However, it means recognizing students as individuals with multifaceted linguistic abilities. Moreover, it requires recognizing that these young people do not come into our classrooms as individuals with zero or minimal reading abilities. They have been educated within the U.S. school system for a number of years and have developed a number of reading practices both inside and outside of school. Yet, their reading practices may not match what is often expected from educators. As demonstrated in the previous chapters, these differences in understanding what type of reading is valued may not be from a lack of learning what was taught in school. In fact, it could be evidence that they developed literacy abilities that were positioned as locally valuable for schooling: listening to the teacher read aloud, copying notes from a PowerPoint slide, and following along on a handout that was being recited by a classmate.

Given what was learned about the in-school reading experiences of the five teenagers that are the focus of this work, in each chapter I included teaching strategies that build upon these complex representations of students' lives and learning experiences. They center the student life experiences, existing abilities, and expand academic opportunity. These themes have been reiterated across this book as fundamental to humanizing reading instruction. Importantly, this book does not purport to provide a one-size-fits all strategies. Instead, it provides a combination of ways of thinking about students' needs and strengths with specific reading strategies to create a pedagogy that can adjust to the context. It rejects the fixation on decontextualized reading strategies that can create dehumanizing pedagogical practices (Bartolomé, 1994; del Carmen Salazar, 2013) As a result, these concrete steps represent actionable change within reading pedagogy that can be applied across content areas. Notably, they respond to the specific findings within this research and dominant trends that have been documented in other studies.

Moving Forward

During the final interview, I asked each of the five teenagers what, if anything, they wanted others to know about them. Destiny told me that nothing in particular came to mind. Eliza felt it was necessary to note that there were different aspects to her identity. For example, sometimes she could be shy and sometimes talkative, but nevertheless, she was always interested in helping other people. Jamilet wanted readers to know that her behavior, or what teachers have characterized as misbehavior, is a reflection of how the person with whom she interacts treats her. Lizbeth wanted to be sure that readers understood that she was a nice person who had goals. One of those significant goals was to become an ultrasound technician. Valeria talked about the importance of Jesus Christ in her life; she wanted people to know that she does make a difference in the world through her actions. It may seem odd to conclude a book about reading pedagogy by describing how the focal students view themselves. However, I made this choice because the fact that they are identified as (long-term) English learners is only one part of who they are as individuals and as students. They were teenagers with multiple experiences, goals, and expectations, who were just preparing to embark on their adult lives. Moving beyond "limited English proficiency" in practice requires that they be treated holistically as individuals rather than being defined by a language policy classification.

Note

1 Reading First was a Federal initiative that was initiated by "No Child Left Behind." Reading First focused on early literacy instruction. Specifically, it emphasized the importance of oral reading fluency for reading instruction. In the school district that the students attended, this resulted in the implementation of scripted reading programs that also focused on oral reading fluency.

REFERENCES

Albright, L. K., & Ariail, M. (2005). Tapping the potential of teacher read-alouds in middle schools. *Journal of Adolescent & Adult Literacy, 48*(7), 582–591.

Alim, H. S. (2010). Critical language awareness. In N. H. Hornberger & S. McKay (Eds.), *Sociolinguistics and language education* (pp. 205–231). Bristol, UK: Multilingual Matters.

Alvarez, S. P., Canagarajah, S., Lee, E., Lee, J. W., & Rabbi, S. (2017). Translingual practice, ethnic identities, and voice in writing. In B. Horner & L. Tetreault (Eds.), *Crossing divides: Exploring translingual writing pedagogies and programs* (pp. 31–47). Boulder, CO: Utah State University Press.

Alvermann, D. E. (2001). Reading adolescents' reading identities: Looking back to see ahead. *Journal of Adolescent & Adult Literacy, 44*(8), 676–690.

Alvermann, D. E. (2006). Struggling adolescent readers: A cultural construction. In A. McKeough, L. Phillips, V. Timmons, & M. Hamilton (Eds.), *Understanding literacy development: A global view* (pp. 95–112). Mahwah, NJ: Lawrence Erlbaum Associates.

Alvermann, D. E. (2018). The optimism of uncertainty: A call to action. *Journal of Adolescent & Adult Literacy, 61*(5), 581–584.

Alvermann, D. E., & Moore, D. W. (1991). Secondary school reading. In R. Barr, L. Kamil, & D. P. Pearson (Eds.), *Handbook of reading research* (pp. 951–983). Mahwah, NJ: Lawrence Erlbaum Associates.

Alvermann, D. E., Young, J. P., Weaver, D., Hinchman, K. A., Moore, D. W., Phelps, S. F. ... Zalewski, P. (1996). Middle and high school students' perceptions of how they experience text-based discussions: A multicase study. *Reading Research Quarterly, 31*(3), 244–267.

Amin, N. (1997). Race and the identity of the nonnative ESL teacher. *TESOL Quarterly, 31*(3), 580–583.

Ariail, M., & Albright, L. K. (2006). A survey of teachers' read-aloud practices in middle schools. *Literacy Research and Instruction, 45*(2), 69–89.

Arlette, I. W. (2015). Literacy and race: Access, equity, and freedom. *Literacy Research: Theory, Method, and Practice, 64*(1), 23–55.

Ascenzi-Moreno, L. (2017). From deficit to diversity: How teachers of recently arrived emergent bilinguals negotiate ideological and pedagogical change. *Schools, 14*(2), 276–302.

Avalos, M. A., Zisselsberger, M., Langer-Osuna, J., & Secada, W. (2015). Building teacher knowledge of academic literacy and language acquisition: A framework for teachers' cross-disciplinary professional learning. In T. Boals, D. Molle, C. A. Hedgspeth, & E. Sato (Eds.), *Multilingual learners and academic literacies* (pp. 267–288). New York, NY: Routledge.

Baker-Bell, A. (2013). "I never really knew the history behind African American language": Critical language pedagogy in an advanced placement English language arts class. *Equity & Excellence in Education, 46*(3), 355–370.

Baker-Bell, A. (2017). "I can switch my language, but I can't switch my skin": What teachers must understand about linguistic racism. In E. Moore, A. Michael & M. W. Penick-Parks (Eds.), *The guide for White women who teach Black boys* (pp. 97–107). Thousand Oaks, CA: Corwin Press.

Balam, O., & de Prada Pérez, A. (2017). Attitudes toward Spanish and code-switching in Belize: Stigmatization and innovation in the Spanish classroom. *Journal of Language, Identity & Education, 16*(1), 17–31.

Balderrama, M. V. (2017). The (mis)preparation of teachers in the Proposition 227 era: Humanizing teacher roles and their practice. *The Urban Review, 33*(3), 255–267.

Ball, A. (2005). Culture and language: Bidialectal issues in literacy. In J. Flood & P. L. Anders (Eds.), *Literacy development of students in urban schools: Research and policy* (pp. 275–287). Newark, DE: International Reading Association.

Barrett, R. (2019). Rewarding language: Language ideology and prescriptive grammar. In V. A. Young, R. Barrett, Y. Young-Rivera, & K. B. Lovejoy (Eds.), *Other people's English: Code-meshing, code-switching, and African American literacy* (pp. 15–23). New York, NY: Routledge.

Bartlett, L. (2007). Bilingual literacies, social identification, and educational trajectories. *Linguistics and Education, 18*(3–4), 215–231.

Bartolomé, L. (1994). Beyond the methods fetish: Toward a humanizing pedagogy. *Harvard Educational Review, 64*(2), 173–195.

Barton, D. (2006). The significance of a social practice view of language, literacy, and numeracy. In L. Tett, M. Hamilton, & Y. Hillier (Eds.), *Adult literacy, numeracy and language: Policy, practice and research* (pp. 21–30). New York, NY: Open University Press.

Barton, D., & Hamilton, M. (2000). Literacy practices. In D. Barton & M. Hamilton (Eds.), *Situated literacies: Reading and writing in context* (pp. 7–15). New York, NY: Routledge.

Baugh, J. (2000). *Beyond ebonics: Linguistic pride and racial prejudice.* Oxford, UK: Oxford University Press.

Bertrand, M., Durand, E. S., & Gonzalez, T. (2017). "We're trying to take action": Transformative agency, role re-mediation, and the complexities of youth participatory action research. *Equity & Excellence in Education, 50*(2), 142–154.

Bloome, D. (2008). Literacies in the classroom. In B. V. Street & N. H. Hornberger (Eds.), *Encyclopedia of language and education: Literacy* (pp. 251–262). New York, NY: Springer.

Borko, H., & Eisenhart, M. (1986). Students' conceptions of reading and their reading experiences in school. *The Elementary School Journal, 86*(5), 589–611.

Brooks, M. D. (2015). "It's like a script": Long-term English learners' experiences with and ideas about academic reading. *Research in the Teaching of English, 49*(4), 383–406.

Brooks, M. D. (2016). Notes and talk: An examination of a long-term English learner reading-to-learn in a high school biology classroom. *Language and Education, 30*(3), 235–251.

Brooks, M. D. (2017). "She doesn't have the basic understanding of a language": Using spelling research to challenge deficit conceptualizations of adolescent bilinguals. *Journal of Literacy Research, 49*(3), 342–370.

Brooks, M. D. (2018). Pushing past myths: Designing instruction for long-term English learners. *TESOL Quarterly, 52*(1), 221–233.

Brooks, M. D. (2019). A mother's advocacy: Lessons for educators of long-term EL students. In H. A. Linville & J. Whiting (Eds.), *Advocacy in English language teaching and learning* (pp. 175–189). New York, NY: Routledge.

Brooks, M. D., & Frankel, K. K. (2018). Oral reading: Practices and purposes in secondary classrooms. *English Teaching: Practice & Critique, 17*(4), 328–341.

Brown, K. (2016). *After the "at-risk" label: Reorienting educational policy and practice*. New York, NY: Teachers College Press.

Brutt-Griffler, J., & Samimy, K. K. (2001). Transcending the nativeness paradigm. *World Englishes, 20*(1), 99–106.

Bryan, K. C. (2016). Making the invisible visible: Immigrant girls of African descent. In P. J. Larke, G. Webb-Hasan, & J. L. Young (Eds.), *Cultivating achievement, respect, and empowerment (CARE) for African American girls in PreK? 12 settings: Implications for access, equity and achievement* (pp. 221–234). Charlotte, NC: IAP.

Bryan, K., Cooper, A., & Ifarinu, B. (2019). From majority to minority: Advocating for English learners from the African Diaspora. In H. A. Linville & J. Whiting (Eds.), *Advocacy in English language teaching and learning* (pp. 190–202). New York, NY: Routledge.

Bunch, G. C., Walqui, A., & Pearson, P. D. (2014). Complex text and new common standards in the United States: Pedagogical implications for English learners. *TESOL Quarterly, 48*(3), 533–559.

Burke, C., Adler, M. A., & Linker, M. (2008). Resisting erasure: Cultivating opportunities for a humanizing curriculum. *Multicultural Perspectives, 10*(2), 65–72.

Busch, B. (2012). The linguistic repertoire revisited. *Applied Linguistics, 33*(5), 503–523.

Callahan, R. M. (2005). Tracking and high school English learners: Limiting opportunity to learn. *American Educational Research Journal, 42*(2), 305–328.

Callahan, R. M., & Shifrer, D. (2016). Equitable access for secondary English learner students: Course taking as evidence of EL program effectiveness. *Educational Administration Quarterly, 52*(3), 463–496.

Chaparro, S. (2014). The communicative burden of making others understand: Why critical language awareness is a must in all ESL (and non-ESL) classrooms. *Working Papers in Education Linguistics, 29*(1), 49–59.

Charity Hudley, A., & Mallinson, C. (2011). *Understanding English language variation in U.S. schools*. New York, NY: Teachers College Press.

Chin, N. B., & Wigglesworth, G. (2007). *Bilingualism: An advanced resource book*. New York, NY: Routledge.

Colón, J. (1961). *Little things are big*. Retrieved from www.facinghistory.org/little-things-are-big-hear-read-story

Cummins, J. (1984). Wanted: A theoretical framework for relating language proficiency to academic achievement among bilingual students. In C. Rivera (Ed.), *Language proficiency and academic achievement* (pp. 2–19). Clevedon, UK: Multilingual Matters.

Czocher, J. A., & Maldonado, L. (2015). A mathematical modeling lens on a conventional word problem. Paper presented at the Annual Meeting of the North American Chapter of the International Group for the Psychology of Mathematics Education, East Lansing, MI, November 5–8.

de la Piedra, M. T. (2011). Adolescent worlds and literacy practices on the United States–Mexico border. *Journal of Adolescent & Adult Literacy, 53*(7), 575–584.

de los Ríos, C. V. (2018). Toward a corridista consciousness: Learning from one transnational youth's critical reading, writing, and performance of Mexican corridos. Reading Research Quarterly, *53*(4), 455–471.

de los Ríos, C. V., & Seltzer, K. (2017). Translanguaging, coloniality, and English classrooms: An exploration of two bicoastal urban classrooms. *Research in the Teaching of English, 52*(1), 55–76.

del Carmen Salazar, M. (2013). A humanizing pedagogy: Reinventing the principles and practice of education as a journey toward liberation. *Review of Research in Education, 37*(1), 121–148.

del Carmen Salazar, M., & Fránquiz, M. E. (2008). The transformation of Ms. Corazon: Creating humanizing spaces for Mexican immigrant students in secondary ESL classrooms. *Multicultural Perspectives, 10*(4), 185–191.

Dillon, D. R., O'Brien, D. G., Moje, E. B., & Stewart, R. A. (2006). Literacy learning in secondary school science classrooms: A cross-case analysis of three qualitative studies. *Journal of Research in Science Teaching, 31*(4), 345–362.

Dorner, L. M., Faulstich Orellana, M., & Jiménez, R. (2008). "It's one of those things that you do to help the family": Language brokering and the development of immigrant adolescents. *Journal of Adolescent Research, 23*(5), 515–543.

Duke, N. K., & Pearson, P. D. (2002). Effective practices for developing reading comprehension. In A. E. Farstrup & S. J. Samuels (Eds.), *What research has to say about reading instruction* (3rd ed., pp. 205–242). Newark, DE: International Reading Association.

Duke, N. K., & Pearson, P. D. (2009). Effective practices for developing reading comprehension. *Journal of Education, 189*(1–2), 107–122.

Duke, N. K., Pearson, D. P., Strachan, S. L., & Billman, A. K. (2011). Essential elements of fostering and teaching reading comprehension. In S. J. Samuels & A. E. Farstrup (Eds.), *What research has to say about reading instruction* (4th ed., pp. 51–93). Newark, DE: International Reading Association.

Durán, L., & Palmer, D. (2014). Pluralist discourses of bilingualism and translanguaging talk in classrooms. *Journal of Early Childhood Literacy, 14*(3), 367–388.

Ede, L., & Lunsford, A. (1984). Audience addressed/audience invoked: The role of audience in composition theory and pedagogy. *College Composition and Communication, 35*(2), 155–171.

Edwards, E., McArthur, S. A., & Russell-Owens, L. (2016). Relationships, being-ness, and voice: Exploring multiple dimensions of humanizing work with black girls. *Equity & Excellence in Education, 49*(4), 428–439.

Elish-Piper, L., Wold, L. S., & Schwingendorf, K. (2014). Scaffolding high school students' reading of complex texts using linked text sets. *Journal of Adolescent & Adult Literacy, 57*(7), 565.

Enriquez, G. (2011). Embodying exclusion: The daily melancholia and performative politics of struggling early adolescent readers. *English Teaching: Practice and Critique, 10*(3), 90–112.

Escamilla, K. (2006). Semilingualism applied to the literacy behaviors of Spanish-speaking emerging bilinguals: Bi-illiteracy or emerging biliteracy? *Teachers College Record, 108*(11), 2329–2353.

Escamilla, K. (2015). Schooling begins before adolescence: The case of Manuel and limited opportunities to learn. In D. Molle, E. Sato, T. Boals, & C. A. Hedgspeth (Eds.), *Multilingual learners and academic literacies: Sociocultural contexts of literacy development in adolescents* (pp. 210–227). New York, NY: Routledge.

Everett, S. (2016). "I just started writing": Toward addressing invisibility, silence, and mortality among academically high-achieving Black male secondary students. *Literacy Research: Theory, Method, and Practice, 65*(1), 316–331.

Faez, F. (2012). Linguistic identities and experiences of generation 1.5 teacher candidates: Race matters. *TESL Canada Journal, 29*, 124.

Faggella-Luby, M., Sampson Graner, P., Deshler, D. D., & Valentino Drew, S. (2012). Building a house on sand: Why disciplinary literacy is not sufficient to replace general strategies for adolescent learners who struggle. *Topics in Language Disorders, 32*(1), 69–84.

Fang, Z. (2008). Going beyond the fab five: Helping students cope with the unique linguistic challenges of expository reading in intermediate grades. *Journal of Adolescent & Adult Literacy, 51*(6), 476–487.

Fang, Z., & Schleppegrell, M. J. (2010). Disciplinary literacies across content areas: Supporting secondary reading through functional language analysis. *Journal of Adolescent & Adult Literacy, 53*(7), 587–597.

Fisher, D., & Frey, N. (2014). *Better learning through structured teaching: A framework for the gradual release of responsibility* (2nd ed.). Alexandria, VA: ASCD.

Flores, N. (2013). Silencing the subaltern: Nation-state/colonial governmentality and bilingual education in the united states. *Critical Inquiry in Language Studies, 10*(4), 263–287.

Flores, N. (2017). The specter of semilingualism in the bilingualism of Latino students. *Texas Education Review, 5*(1), 76–80.

Flores, N., Kleyn, T., & Menken, K. (2015). Looking holistically in a climate of partiality: Identities of students labeled long-term English language learners. *Journal of Language, Identity & Education, 14*(2), 113–132.

Flores, N., & Rosa, J. D. (2015). Undoing appropriateness: Raciolinguistic ideologies and language diversity in education. *Harvard Educational Review, 85*(2), 149–171.

Flores, T. T. (2018). Chicas fuertes: Counterstories of Latinx parents raising strong girls. *Bilingual Research Journal, 41*(3), 329–348.

Fought, C. (2003). *Chicano English in context*. New York, NY: Palgrave Macmillan.

Frankel, K. K. (2016). The intersection of reading and identity in high school literacy intervention classes. *Research in the Teaching of English, 51*(1), 37–59.

Frankel, K. K. (2017). What does it mean to be a reader? identity and positioning in two high school literacy intervention classes. *Reading & Writing Quarterly, 33*(6), 501–518.

Frankel, K. K., Becker, B. L. C., Rowe, M. W., & Pearson, P. D. (2016). From "what is reading?" to what is literacy? *Journal of Education, 196*(3), 7–17.

Frankel, K. K., & Brooks, M. D. (2018). Why the "struggling reader" label is harmful (and what educators can do about it). *Journal of Adolescent & Adult Literacy, 62*(1), 111–114.

Frankel, K. K., & Fields, S. S. (2019). Disrupting storylines: A case study of one adolescent's identity, agency, and positioning during literacy tutoring. *Literacy Research and Instruction, 58*(3), 142–163.

Fránquiz, M. E., & del Carmen Salazar, M. (2004). The transformative potential of humanizing pedagogy: Addressing the diverse needs of Chicano/Mexicano students. *The High School Journal, 87*(4), 36–53.

Franzak, J. K. (2006). Zoom: A review of the literature on marginalized adolescent readers, literacy theory, and policy implications. *Review of Educational Research, 76*(2), 209–248.

Freeman, Y. S., Freeman, D. E., & Mercuri, S. (2002). *Closing the achievement gap: How to reach limited-formal-schooling and long-term English learners*. Portsmouth, NH: Heinemann.

Freire, P. (1984). *Pedagogy of the oppressed*. New York, NY: Bergin & Garvey.

Gándara, P., & Escamilla, K. (2017). Bilingual education in the United States. In O. García, A. Lin, & S. May (Eds.), *Bilingual and multilingual education* (pp. 1–14). New York, NY: Springer International.

Garcia, A. (2012). Adventures with text and beyond: "Like reading" and literacy challenges in a digital age. *The English Journal, 101*(6), 93–96.

García, O. (2009). Emergent bilinguals and TESOL: What's in a name? *TESOL Quarterly, 43*(2), 322–326.

García, O., & Wei, L. (2014). *Translanguaging and education*. London, UK: Palgrave MacMillan.

García-Sánchez, I. (2016). Multiculturalism and its discontents: Essentializing ethnic Moroccan and Roma identities in classroom discourse in Spain. In H. Samy Alim, J. R. Rickford, & A. F. Ball (Eds.), *Raciolinguistics: How language shapes our ideas about race* (pp. 291–308). Oxford, UK: Oxford University Press.

Gay, I., & Karen, B. (2011). "Just plain reading": A survey of what makes students want to read in middle school classrooms. *Reading Research Quarterly, 36*(4), 350–377.

Gee, J. P. (2003). Opportunity to learn: A language-based perspective on assessment. *Assessment in Education: Principles, Policy & Practice, 10*(1), 27–46.

Gee, J. P. (2004). *Situated language and learning: A critique of traditional schooling*. New York, NY: Routledge.

Gerson, D. (2016). How do you teach English to Americans? *LA Times*. Retrieved from www.latimes.com/local/education/la-me-english-learners-moreno-valley-20160418-story.html

Glenn, W. J., & Ginsberg, R. (2016). Resisting readers' identity (re)construction across English and young adult literature course contexts. *Research in the Teaching of English, 51*(1), 84.

Glossary of Education Reform (2015). Long-term English learner. Retrieved from www.edglossary.org/long-term-english-learner

Golden, N. A., & Womack, E. (2016). Cultivating literacy and relationships with adolescent scholars of color. *English Journal, 105*(3), 36–42.

Goldenberg, C., & Rutherford-Quach, S. (2012). The Arizona home language survey: The under-identification of students for English language services. *Language Policy, 11*(1), 21–30.

Goldman, S. R., & Rakestraw, J. A. (2000). Structural aspects of constructing meaning from a text. In M. L. Kamil, P. B. Mosenthal, P. D. Pearson, & R. Barr (Eds.), *Handbook of reading research* (Vol. 3, pp. 311–336). Mahwah, NJ: Lawrence Erlbaum Associates.

Gomez, M. L. (2004). Textual tactics of identification. *Anthropology & Education Quarterly, 35*(4), 391–410.

Gort, M. (2012). Code-switching patterns in the writing-related talk of young emergent bilinguals. *Journal of Literacy Research, 44*(1), 45–75.

Gort, M., & Sembiante, S. F. (2015). Navigating hybridized language learning spaces through translanguaging pedagogy: Dual language preschool teachers' languaging practices in support of emergent bilingual children's performance of academic discourse. *International Multilingual Research Journal, 9*(1), 7–25.

Green, L. (2002). *African American English: A linguistic introduction*. Cambridge, UK: Cambridge University Press.

Greene, D. T. (2016). "We need more 'US' in schools!!" Centering black adolescent girls' literacy and language practices in online school spaces. *The Journal of Negro Education, 85*(3), 274–289.

Greenleaf, C., Schoenbach, R., Cziko, C., & Mueller, F. (2001). Apprenticing adolescent readers to academic literacy. *Harvard Educational Review, 71*(1), 79–130.

Greenleaf, C., & Valencia, S. W. (2017). Missing in action: Learning from texts in subject-matter classrooms. In K. A. Hinchman & D. Appleman (Eds.), *Adolescent literacies: A handbook of practice-based research* (pp. 235–256). New York, NY: Guilford Press.

Grosjean, F. (2008). *Studying bilinguals*. Oxford, UK: Oxford University Press.

Guthrie, J. T., & Klauda, S. L. (2014). Effects of classroom practices on reading comprehension, engagement, and motivations for adolescents. *Reading Research Quarterly, 49*(4), 387–416.

Gutiérrez, K. D., Morales, P. Z., & Martinez, D. C. (2009). Re-mediating literacy: Culture, difference, and learning for students from nondominant communities. *Review of Research in Education, 33*(1), 212–245.

Haas, E., & Gort, M. (2009). Demanding more: Legal standards and best practices for English language learners. *Bilingual Research Journal, 32*(2), 115–135.

Haddix, M. (2011). Black boys can write: Challenging dominant framings of African American adolescent males in literacy research. *Journal of Adolescent & Adult Literacy, 53*(4), 341–343.

Haddix, M., & Sealey-Ruiz, Y. (2012). Cultivating digital and popular literacies as empowering and emancipatory acts among urban youth. *Journal of Adolescent & Adult Literacy, 56*(3), 189–192.

Hall, J. K., Cheng, A., & Carlson, M. T. (2006). Reconceptualizing multicompetence as a theory of language knowledge. *Applied Linguistics, 27*(2), 220–240.

Hall, L. A. (2012). The role of reading identities and reading abilities in students' discussions about texts and comprehension strategies. *Journal of Literacy Research, 44*(3), 239–272.

Hall, L. A. (2016). The role of identity in reading comprehension development. *Reading & Writing Quarterly, 32*(1), 56–80.

Halliday, M. A. K., & Hasan, R. (1976). *Cohesion in English*. London, UK: Longman.

Hartman, J. A., & Hartman, D. K. (1994). *Arranging multi-text reading experiences that expand the reader's role (technical report no. 604)*. Champaign, IL: Center for the Study of Reading.

Hernandez, S. J. (2017). Are they all language learners?: Educational labeling and raciolinguistic identifying in a California middle school dual language program. *CATESOL Journal, 29*(1), 133–154.

Hiebert, E. H., Wilson, K. M., & Trainin, G. (2010). Are students really reading in independent reading contexts? An examination of comprehension-based silent reading rate. In E. H. Hiebert & D. R. Reutzel (Eds.), *Revisiting silent reading: New directions for teachers and researchers* (pp. 58–77). Newark, DE: International Reading Association.

Hinchman, K. (1987). The textbook and three content-area teachers. *Reading Research and Instruction, 26*(4), 247–263.

Hinchman, K., Alvermann, D. E., Boyd, F. B., Brozo, W. G., & Vacca, R. T. (2003). Supporting older students' in- and out-of-school literacies. *Journal of Adolescent & Adult Literacy, 47*(4), 304–310.

Hull, G. A., & Moje, E. B. (2012). What is the development of literacy the development of? In K. Hakuta & M. Santos (Eds.), Commissioned papers on language and literacy issues in the Common Core State Standards and Next Generation Science Standards (pp. 52–63). Retrieved from https://mes.sccoe.org/depts/ell/13th%20Annual%20Accountability%20Leadership%20Institute/11_KenjiUL%20Stanford%20Final%205-9-12%20w%20cover.pdf#page=64

Ibrahim, A. E. K. M. (1999). Becoming Black: Rap and hip-hop, race, gender, identity, and the politics of ESL learning. *TESOL Quarterly, 33*(3), 349–369.

Irizarry, J. G. (2017). "For us, by us": A vision of culturally sustaining pedagogies forwarded by Latinx youth. In D. Paris & H. Samy Alim (Eds.), *Culturally sustaining pedagogies: Teaching and learning for justice in a changing world* (pp. 83–98). New York, NY: Teachers College Press.

Irizarry, J. G., & Brown, T. M. (2014). Humanizing research in dehumanizing spaces: The challenges and opportunities of conducting participatory action research with youth in schools. In D. Paris & M. T. Winn (Eds.), *Humanizing research: Decolonizing qualitative inquiry with youth and communities* (pp. 63–80). Thousand Oaks, CA: Sage Publications.

Ivey, G., & Broaddus, K. (2001). "Just plain reading": A survey of what makes students want to read in middle school classrooms. *Reading Research Quarterly, 36*(4), 350–377.

Jiménez, R. T., García, G. E., & Pearson, P. D. (1996). The reading strategies of bilingual Latina/o students who are successful English readers: Opportunities and obstacles. *Reading Research Quarterly, 31*(1), 90–112.

Jiménez, R. T., David, S., Fagan, K., Risko, V. J., Pacheco, M., Pray, L., & Gonzales, M. (2015). Using translation to drive conceptual development for students becoming literate in English as an additional language. *Research in the Teaching of English, 49*(3), 248.

Joseph, N. M., Hailu, M. F., & Matthews, J. S. (2019). Normalizing Black girls' humanity in mathematics classrooms. *Harvard Educational Review, 89*(1), 132–155.

Kamhi-Stein, L. D. (2003). Reading in two languages: How attitudes toward home language and beliefs about reading affect the behaviors of "underprepared" L2 college readers. *TESOL Quarterly, 37*(1), 35–71.

Karam, F. J. (2018). Language and identity construction: The case of a refugee digital bricoleur. *Journal of Adolescent and Adult Literacy, 61*(5), 511–521.

Kibler, A. K., Karam, F. J., Futch Ehrlich, V. A., Bergey, R., Wang, C., & Molloy Elreda, L. (2017). Who are "long-term English learners"? Using classroom interactions to deconstruct a manufactured learner label. *Applied Linguistics, 39*(5), 741–765.

Kibler, A. K., & Valdés, G. (2016). Conceptualizing language learners: Socioinstitutional mechanisms and their consequences. *The Modern Language Journal, 100*(S1), 96–116.

Kim, W. G., & García, S. B. (2014). Long-term English language learners' perceptions of their language and academic learning experiences. *Remedial and Special Education, 35*(5), 300–312.

King, K., & Bigelow, M. (2016). The language policy of placement tests for newcomer English learners. *Educational Policy, 32*(7), 936–968.

Kinloch, V. F. (2005). Revisiting the promise of "students' right to their own language": Pedagogical strategies. *College Composition and Communication, 57*(1), 83–113.

Kinloch, V., Burkhard, T., & Penn, C. (2017). When school is not enough: Understanding the lives and literacies of Black youth. *Research in the Teaching of English, 52*(1), 34.

Kiramba, L. K. (2017). Multilingual literacies: Invisible representation of literacy in a rural classroom. *Journal of Adolescent & Adult Literacy, 61*(3), 267–277.

Klecker, B. M., & Pollock, M. A. (2005). Congruency of research-based literacy instruction in high and low performing schools. *Reading Improvement, 42*(3), 149–158.

Kleyn, T., & Stern, N. (2018). Labels as limitations. *Writing, 34*. Retrieved from http://minnetesoljournal.org/spring-2018/labels-as-limitations

Ladson-Billings, G. (1995). Toward a theory of culturally relevant pedagogy. *American Educational Research Journal, 32*(3), 465–491.

Ladson-Billings, G. (2014). Culturally relevant pedagogy 2.0: A.k.a. the remix. *Harvard Educational Review, 84*(1), 74–84.

Lam, W. S. E. (2009). Multiliteracies on instant messaging in negotiating local, translocal, and transnational affiliations: A case of an adolescent immigrant. *Reading Research Quarterly, 44*(4), 377–397.

Learned, J. E. (2016). "The behavior kids" examining the conflation of youth reading difficulty and behavior problem positioning among school institutional contexts. *American Educational Research Journal, 53*(5), 1271–1309.

Learned, J. E., Morgan, M. J., & Lui, A. M. (2019). "Everyone's voices are to be heard": A comparison of struggling and proficient readers' perspectives in one urban high school. *Education and Urban Society, 51*(2), 195–221.

Lee, C. D., & Spratley, A. (2010). *Reading in the disciplines: The challenges of adolescent literacy.* New York, NY: Carnegie.

Lesaux, N. K., & Geva, E. (2006). Synthesis: Development of literacy in language-minority students. In D. Auugust, & T. Shanahan (Eds.), *Developing literacy in second-language learners: Report of the national literacy panel on language minority children and youth* (pp. 53–74). Mahwah, NJ: Lawrence Erlbaum Associates.

Leung, C., Harris, R., & Rampton, B. (1997). The idealised native speaker, reified ethnicities, and classroom realities. *TESOL Quarterly, 31*(3), 543–560.

Lewis, C., Enciso, P. E., & Moje, E. B. (Eds.). (2007). *Reframing sociocultural research on literacy: Identity, agency, and power.* New York, NY: Routledge.

Lewis Ellison, T. (2017). Digital participation, agency, and choice: An African American youth's digital storytelling about Minecraft. *Journal of Adolescent & Adult Literacy, 61*(1), 25–35.

Lippi-Green, R. (2012). *English with an accent: Language, ideology, and discrimination in the United States.* New York, NY: Routledge.

Lo, A. (2016). Suddenly faced with a Chinese village? The linguistic racialization of Asian Americans. In H. S. Alim, J. R. Rickford, & A. Ball (Eds.), *Raciolinguistics: How language shapes our ideas about race* (pp. 97–111). New York, NY: Oxford University Press.

Lupo, S. M., Strong, J. Z., Lewis, W., Walpole, S., & McKenna, M. C. (2018). Building background knowledge through reading: Rethinking text sets. *Journal of Adolescent and Adult Literacy, 61*(4), 433–444.

MacSwan, J. (2017). A multilingual perspective on translanguaging. *American Educational Research Journal, 54*(1), 167–201.

Makoni, S., & Pennycook, A. (Eds.). (2007). *Disinventing and reconstituting languages.* Clevedon, UK: Multilingual Matters.

Martinez, D. C. (2016). Latino linguistic repertoires in an intensely-segregated black and Latina/o high school: Is this super-diversity? *International Journal of the Sociology of Language, 2016*(241), 69–95.

Martínez, R. A. (2010). "Spanglish" as literacy tool: Toward an understanding of the potential role of Spanish-English code-switching in the development of academic literacy. *Research in the Teaching of English, 45*(2), 124–149.

Martínez, R. A., Hikida, M., & Durán, L. (2015). Unpacking ideologies of linguistic purism: How dual language teachers make sense of everyday translanguaging. *International Multilingual Research Journal, 9*(1), 26–42.

Mason, L., Scirica, F., & Salvi, L. (2006). Effects of beliefs about meaning construction and task instructions on interpretation of narrative text. *Contemporary Educational Psychology, 31*(4), 411–437.

Maxwell, L. A. (2012). California governor approves long-term ELL bill. *Learning the Language* (Education Week's Blogs). Retrieved from http://blogs.edweek.org/edweek/learning-the-language/2012/09/california_governor_approves_l.html

McDermott, R., & Varenne, H. (1995). Culture as disability. *Anthropology & Education Quarterly, 26*(3), 324–348.

McNamara, T., Khan, K., & Frost, K. (2015). Language tests for residency and citizenship and the conferring of individuality. In B. Spolsky, O. Inbar-Lourie & M. Tannenbaum (Eds.), *Challenges for language education and policy: Making space for people* (pp. 11–22). New York, NY: Routledge.

McTighe, J., Seif, E., & Wiggins, G. (2004). You can teach for meaning. *Educational Leadership, 62*(1), 26–30.

Menken, K. (2013). Emergent bilingual students in secondary school: Along the academic language and literacy continuum. *Language Teaching, 46*(4), 438–476.

Menken, K., & García, O. (2010). *Negotiating language education policies: Educators as policymakers.* New York, NY: Routledge.

Menken, K., & Kleyn, T. (2009). The difficult road for long-term English learners. *Educational Leadership, 66*(7), 26–29.

Menken, K., & Kleyn, T. (2010). The long-term impact of subtractive schooling in the educational experiences of secondary English language learners. *International Journal of Bilingual Education and Bilingualism, 13*(4), 399–417.

Menken, K., Kleyn, T., & Chae, N. (2012). Spotlight on "long-term English language learners": Characteristics and prior schooling experiences of an invisible population. *International Multilingual Research Journal, 6*(2), 121–142.

Milner, H. R. (2012). But what is urban education? *Urban Education, 47*(3), 556–561.

Morales, P. Z. (2016). Transnational practices and language maintenance: Spanish and Zapoteco in California. *Children's Geographies, 14*(4), 375–389.

Mosqueda, E., Bravo, M., Solís, J., Maldonado, S. I., & De La Rosa, J. (2016). Preparing middle school students for the transition to high school mathematics: Assessing Latinas/os' mathematical understanding, academic language and English proficiency. *Bilingual Review/Revista Bilingüe, 33*(2), 1–20.

Motha, S. (2014). *Race, empire, and English language teaching: Creating responsible and ethical anti-racist practice.* New York, NY: Teachers College Press.

Neuman, M., & Rao, S. (2004). Adolescent literacy: Beyond English class, beyond decoding text. *Voices in Urban Education, Winter/Spring, 3*, 6–13.

Nyachae, T. M. (2019). Social justice literacy workshop for critical dialogue. *Journal of Adolescent & Adult Literacy, 63*(1), 106–110.

Obeng, S., & Obeng, C. (2006). African immigrant families' views on English as a Second Language (ESL) classes held for newly arrived immigrant children in the united states elementary and middle schools: A study in ethnography. In M. Firmin & P. Brewer (Eds.), *Ethnographic and qualitative research in education* (pp. 105–116). Newcastle, UK: Cambridge Scholars Press.

O'Brien, D., Beach, R., & Scharber, C. (2007). "Struggling" middle schoolers: Engagement and literate competence in a reading writing intervention class. *Reading Psychology, 28*(1), 51–73.

Olsen, L. (2010). *Reparable harm: Fulfilling the unkept promise of educational opportunity for California's long term English learners.* Long Beach, CA: Californians Together.

Olsen, L. (2014). *Meeting the unique needs of long term English language learners: A guide for educators.* Washington, DC: National Education Association.

Orwell, G. (2010). *Animal farm*. New York, NY: Random House.

Otheguy, R., García, O., & Reid, W. (2015). Clarifying translanguaging and deconstructing named languages: A perspective from linguistics. *Applied Linguistics Review, 6*(3), 281–307.

Palincsar, A. S., & Duke, N. K. (2004). The role of text and text-reader interactions in young children's reading development and achievement. *Elementary School Journal, 105*(2), 183–197.

Paris, D. (2012). Culturally sustaining pedagogy: A needed change in stance, terminology, and practice. *Educational Researcher, 41*(3), 93–97.

Paris, D., & Alim, H. S. (2014). What are we seeking to sustain through culturally sustaining pedagogy? A loving critique forward. *Harvard Educational Review, 84*(1), 85–100.

Patterson, A., Roman, D., Friend, M., Osborne, J., & Donovan, B. (2018). Reading for meaning: The foundational knowledge every teacher of science should have. *International Journal of Science Education, 40*(3), 291–307.

Pearson, P. D., & Hiebert, E. H. (2014). The state of the field: Qualitative analyses of text complexity. *Elementary School Journal, 115*(2), 161–183.

Pearson, P. D., & Gallagher, M. C. (1983). The instruction of reading comprehension. *Contemporary Educational Psychology, 8*(3), 317–344.

Pease-Alvarez, L. (2002). Moving beyond linear trajectories of language shift and bilingual language socialization. *Hispanic Journal of Behavioral Sciences, 24*(2), 114–137.

Penfield, J. (1983). The vernacular base of literacy development in Chicano English. In J. Ornstein-Galicia (Ed.), *Form and function in Chicano English* (pp. 71–83). Rowley, MA: Newberry House.

Phelps, S. (2005). *Ten years of research on adolescent literacy, 1994–2004: A review*. Naperville, IL: Learning Point Associates.

Poza, L. E. (2018). The language of ciencia: Translanguaging and learning in a bilingual science classroom. *International Journal of Bilingual Education and Bilingualism, 21*(1), 1–19.

Pressley, M., & Afflerbach, P. (1995). *Verbal protocols of reading: The nature of constructively responsive reading*. Mahwah, NJ: Lawrence Erlbaum and Associates.

Protacio, M. S., & Jang, B. G. (2016). ESL teachers' perceptions about English learners' reading motivation. *Literacy Research: Theory, Method, and Practice, 65*(1), 166–181.

Reyes, M., & Domina, T. (2019). A mixed-methods study: Districts' implementation of language classification policies and the implications for male, Hispanic, and low-income middle school students. *Education Policy Analysis Archives, 27*, 30.

Rickford, J. R., & Rickford, R. J. (2000). *Spoken soul: The story of Black English*. New York, NY: Wiley.

Romaine, S. (1995). *Bilingualism* (2nd ed.). Oxford, UK: Blackwell.

Rosa, J. (2016). Standardization, racialization, languagelessness: Raciolinguistic ideologies across communicative contexts. *Journal of Linguistic Anthropology, 26*(2), 162–183.

Rosa, J. (2019). *Looking like a language, sounding like a race*. New York, NY: Oxford University Press.

Rosario-Ramos, E. M. (2018). "Why aren't there enough of our stories to read?" teaching autoethnographies for radical healing. *English Teaching: Practice & Critique, 17*(3), 213–227.

Rosenblatt, L. (1994). The transactional theory of reading and writing. In R. B. Ruddell, M. R. Ruddell, & H. Singer (Eds.), *Theoretical models and processes of reading* (pp. 1057–1092). Newark, DE: International Reading Association.

Rubinstein-Ávila, E. (2003). Conversing with Miguel: An adolescent English language learner struggling with later literacy development. *Journal of Adolescent & Adult Literacy, 47*(4), 290–301.

Rubinstein-Ávila, E. (2007). From the Dominican Republic to drew high: What counts as literacy for Yanira Lara? *Reading Research Quarterly, 42*(4), 568–589.

Sahakyan, N., & Ryan, S. (2018). *Exploring the long-term English learner population across 15 WIDA states (WIDA research report no. RR-2018-1).* Madison, WI: WIDA at the Wisconsin Center for Education Research.

Salerno, A. S., & Kibler, A. K. (2016). "This group of difficult kids": The discourse pre-service English teachers use to label students. *Journal of Education for Students Placed at Risk (JESPAR), 21*(4), 261–278.

Santa Ana, A. O. (1993). Chicano English and the nature of the Chicano language setting. *Hispanic Journal of Behavioral Sciences, 15,* 3.

Santiago, M. (2019). Historical inquiry to challenge the narrative of racial progress. *Cognition and Instruction, 37*(1), 93–117.

Scarcella, R. (2003). *Academic English: A conceptual framework.* eScholarship, University of California. Retrieved from www.openaire.eu/search/publication?articleId=od_____ _325::888660c45a7f0a9727b19c1d3497bd4f

Schissel, J. L., & Kangas, S. E. (2018). Reclassification of emergent bilinguals with disabilities: The intersectionality of improbabilities. *Language Policy, 17*(4), 567–589.

Schoenbach, R., Greenleaf, C., & Murphy, L. (2012). *Reading for understanding: How reading apprenticeship improves disciplinary learning in secondary and college classrooms* (2nd ed.). San Francisco, CA: Jossey-Bass.

Schraw, G. (2000). Reader beliefs and meaning construction in narrative text. *Journal of Educational Psychology, 92*(1), 96.

Sciurba, K. (2017). Journeys toward textual relevance: Male readers of color and the significance of Malcolm X and Harry Potter. *Journal of Literacy Research, 49*(3), 371–392.

Shanahan, T., & Shanahan, C. (2008). Teaching disciplinary literacy to adolescents: Rethinking content- area literacy. *Harvard Educational Review, 78*(1), 40–59.

Shanahan, T., & Shanahan, C. (2012). What is disciplinary literacy and why does it matter? *Topics in Language Disorders, 32*(1), 7–18.

Skerrett, A. (2012). "We hatched in this class": Repositioning of identity in and beyond a reading classroom. *The High School Journal, 95*(3), 62–75.

Skerrett, A. (2014). Religious literacies in a secular literacy classroom. *Reading Research Quarterly, 49*(2), 233–250.

Smagorinsky, P. (2001a). If meaning is constructed, what is it made from? Toward a cultural theory of reading. *Review of Educational Research, 71*(1), 133–169.

Smagorinsky, P. (2001b). Rethinking protocol analysis from a cultural perspective. *Annual Review of Applied Linguistics, 21,* 233–245.

Smith, B. E., Pacheco, M. B., & Rossato de Almeida, C. (2017). Multimodal codemeshing: Bilingual adolescents' processes composing across modes and languages. *Journal of Second Language Writing, 36,* 6–22.

Smith, P. (2019). "How does a Black person speak English?" Beyond American language norms. *American Educational Research Journal,* doi:0002831219850760.

Snow, C. E., & Biancarosa, G. (2003). *Adolescent literacy and the achievement gap: What do we know and where do we go from here?* New York, NY: Carnegie Corporation.

Souto-Manning, M. (2017). Generative text sets: Tools for negotiating critically inclusive early childhood teacher education pedagogical practices. *Journal of Early Childhood Teacher Education, 38*(1), 79–101.

Stewart, M. A. (2014). Social networking, workplace, and entertainment literacies: The out-of-school literate lives of newcomer adolescent immigrants. *Literacy Research and Instruction, 53*(4), 347–371.

Street, B.V. (1984). *Literacy in theory and practice*. New York, NY: Cambridge.

Street, B.V. (2008). New literacies, new times: Development in literacy studies. In B.V. Street & N. Hornberger (Eds.), *Literacy: Encyclopdeia of language and education* (Vol. 2, pp. 3–14). New York, NY: Springer.

Street, B.V. (2012). New literacy studies. In M. Grenfell, D. Bloome, C. Hardy, K. Pahl, J. Roswell, & B.V. Street (Eds.), *Language, ethnography, and education: Bridging new literacy studies and Bourdieu* (pp. 27–49). New York, NY: Routledge.

Sturtevant, E. G., Boyd, F. B., Brozo, W. G., Hinchman, K. A., Moore, D. W., & Alvermann, D. E. (2016). *Principled practices for adolescent literacy: A framework for instruction and policy*. New York, NY: Routledge.

Swanson, E., Wanzek, J., McCulley, L., Stillman-Spisak, S., Vaughn, S., Simmons, D. ... Hairrell, A. (2016). Literacy and text reading in middle and high school social studies and English language arts classrooms. *Reading & Writing Quarterly, 32*(3), 199–222.

Tatum, A. (2008). Toward a more anatomically complete model of literacy instruction: A focus on African American male adolescents and texts. *Harvard Educational Review, 78*(1), 155–180.

Thompson, K. D. (2015). Questioning the long-term English learner label: How categorization can blind us to students' abilities. *Teachers College Record, 117*(12), 1–50.

Tuck, E. (2009). Suspending damage: A letter to communities. *Harvard Educational Review, 79*(3), 409–428.

Uno, R. (2011). *Hurler's syndrome*. Retrieved from www.buzzle.com/articles/hurlers-syndrome.html

U.S. Department of Education. (2016). *Non-regulatory guidance: English learners and Title III of the elementary and secondary education act (ESEA), as amended by the Every Student Succeeds Act (ESSA)*. Washington, DC: U.S. Department of Education. Retrieved from www2.ed.gov/policy/elsec/leg/essa/essatitleiiiguidenglishlearners92016.pdf

Valdés, G. (2001). *Learning and not learning English: Latino students in American schools*. New York, NY: Teachers College.

Valdés, G. (2017). From language maintenance and intergenerational transmission to language survivance: Will "heritage language" education help or hinder? *International Journal of the Sociology of Language, 2017*(243), 67–95.

Valdés, G., & Figueroa, R. (1994). *Bilingualism and testing: A special case of bias*. Norwood, NJ: Ablex.

Valdés, G., Lomelí, K., Taube, J., & Teachers of Latino College Preparatory Academy. (2017). Nurturing discursive strengths: Efforts to improve the teaching of reading and writing in a Latino charter school. In R. K. Durst, G. E. Newell & J. D. Marshall (Eds.), *English language arts research and teaching: Revisiting and extending Arthur Applebee's contributions* (pp. 107–122). New York, NY: Routledge Press.

Valdés, G., MacSwan, J., & Alvarez, L. (2009). Deficits and differences: Perspectives on language and education. Paper presented at the National Academy of Sciences Workshop on the Role of Language in School Learning: Implications for Closing the Achievement Gap, Menlo Park, CA.

Valdés, G., Poza, L. E., & Brooks, M. D. (2014). Educating students who do not speak the societal language: The social construction of language learner categories. *Profession*. Retrieved from https://profession.mla.hcommons.org/2014/10/09/educating-students-who-do-not-speak-the-societal-language/

Valdés, G., Poza, L. E., & Brooks, M. D. (2015). Language acquisition in bilingual education. In W. E. Wright, S. Boun, & O. García (Eds.), *The handbook of bilingual and multilingual education* (pp. 56–74). Malden, MA: John Wiley & Sons.

Villaseñor, V. (2008). *Burro genius: A memoir.* New York, NY: HarperCollins.

Wade, S., & Moje, E. (2000). The role of text in classroom learning. In M. L. Kamil, P. B. Mosenthal, D. P. Pearson & R. Barr (Eds.), *Handbook of reading research* (pp. 609–628). Mahwah, NJ: Lawrence Erlbaum Associates.

Watanabe, T. (2014). California schools step up efforts to help "long-term English learners." *The Los Angeles Times.* Retrieved from www.latimes.com/local/education/la-me-english-learners-20141218-story.html

Wiesel, E., & Wiesel, M. (2006). *Night.* New York, NY: Hill and Wang.

Willis, A. I. (2007). *Reading comprehension research and testing in the U.S.: Undercurrents of race, class, and power in the struggle for meaning.* New York, NY: Routledge Press.

Willis, A. I. (2015). Literacy and race: Access, equity, and freedom. *Literacy Research: Theory, Method, and Practice, 64*(1), 23–55.

Wilson, A., Madjar, I., & McNaughton, S. (2016). Opportunity to learn about disciplinary literacy in senior secondary English classrooms in New Zealand. *The Curriculum Journal, 27*(2), 204–228.

Wright, R. (2007). *Black boy.* New York, NY: Harper Perennial Modern Classics.

Young, V. A. (2009). "Nah, we straight": An argument against code switching. *Jac, 29*(1–2), 49–76.

Zapata, A., & Laman, T. T. (2016). "I write to show how beautiful my languages are": Translingual writing instruction in English-dominant classrooms. *Language Arts, 93*(5), 366–378.

Zehr, M. A. (2010). Home-language surveys for ELLs under fire. *Education Week.* Retrieved from www.edweek.org/ew/articles/2010/02/16/22homelanguage_ep.h29. html?tkn=POLFZ/PsWLFT5/ UXkwYJ2FJYWJYImD4uagUF&cmp=clp-edweek

Zentella, A. C. (1997). *Growing up bilingual: Puerto Rican children in New York.* Malden, MA: Blackwell Publishers.

INDEX